Walking in the
Conwy Valley

Walking in the
Conwy Valley

15 circular walks in and around the Vale of Conwy—from Betws-y-Coed to the Great Orme

Carl Rogers

Mara Publications

First published in June 1997 by **Mara Publications**,
22 Crosland Terrace, Helsby, Cheshire WA6 9LY.

All enquiries regarding sales, telephone: (01928) 723744

ISBN 0 9522409 7 1

Acknowledgements
I would like to say thank you to the following
individuals for their help in preparing this book: Jack
Rogers for checking all the routes along with Audrey
Rogers, Richard Evans, David Telfor and Martin
Ogden; Chris Mitchell for proofing the text.

Cover photographs: front—the Crafnant valley
                    back—Moel Siabod and Snowdon from Capel Garmon

Layout and design by Mara Publications.
Text, maps and photographs © Carl Rogers 1997

British Library Cataloguing-in-publication data.
A catalogue is available for this book from the British Library.

Sketch maps based on the Ordnance Survey 1:25, 000 map with the
permission of the Controller of HM Stationary Office.

Printed and bound by MFP Design & Print, telephone 0161-864 4540

Contents

		Page
Introduction		6
History		10
Map		21
Glossary of Welsh names		22
1	The Great Orme 5 miles	24
2	The Little Orme 4¾ miles	29
3	Conwy Mountain 6½ miles	34
4	Capelulo 6¼ miles	42
5	Rowen 3¾ miles	47
6	Caerhun 3½ miles	52
7	Dolgarrog 5 miles	57
8	Maenan 3 miles	61
9	Trefriw and Llanrwst 5½ miles	65
10	Llyn Crafnant 5 miles	71
11	Betws y Coed—Llyn Parc 4½ miles	76
12	Betws y Coed—Llyn Elsi 3¾ miles	81
13	Moel Trefriw 2¾ miles	86
14	Capel Garmon 4½ miles	90
15	Machno Falls 5 miles	94

Introduction

From its source on the flat moors of Migneint to its discharge into Conwy Bay at Deganwy, Afon Conwy is a little under 30 miles long, yet in this short journey it flows through one of North Wales' most significant river valleys—Dyffryn Conwy.

The valley owes its present form to the action of ancient glaciers moving north from the Snowdonian highlands. This has resulted in a deep fjord-like valley which reaches inland for over 15 miles and has, in effect, extended the fertile coastal plain into the heart of the mountains. Because of this, the valley has long been settled and has been at the centre of North Wales' history for almost 1,500 years. Here also, the soft contours of the Denbigh Moors meet the rugged terrain of Snowdonia. This dramatic change in the landscape can be explained by the presence of a geological fault—a line of weakness which the forces of water and ice were able to exploit.

The glacial origin of the valley has given it typical 'U' shaped characteristics with steep and often precipitous valley sides rising above a flat fertile floor. For much of its history the floor of the valley was washed by shallow tidal waters, which along with silt brought down by the river, has resulted in the build up of rich alluvial soils. Because of this and because such flat land is rare in this part of Wales, it has been extensively farmed since the early Middle Ages. In its lower reaches below Tal-y-Cafn, the river is still broad with extensive tidal sands, although Thomas Telford's bridge and causeway across the mouth of the river have greatly accelerated the rate of siltation and spread of spartia marsh grass.

To the west of this divide lies a high plateau about 700-900 feet above the valley floor. From here long glacial valleys lead up to the highest summits of the Carneddau range. The legacy of a long settlement in this area is apparent in the numerous ancient trackways, ruined farms and prehistoric remains still to be seen. To the east, softer contours and lower altitudes have given rise to a more cultivated landscape of sheep grazed fields and dry-stone walls. A myriad of narrow country lanes connect a handful of small villages and offer unrivalled views of Snowdonia's highest peaks.

The northern end of the valley is quite different. Again this change is due to the underlying geology. Here a band of carboniferous limestone has been weathered into a series of low hills and exposed headlands; the most famous being the Great Orme. Heavily populated in the past and increasingly

Moel Siabod and Snowdon from above Capel Garmon

The exposed landscape of the Great Orme above Llandudno

so today, the Great Orme and its neighbours are justifiably popular, giving wide panoramas inland to the mountains and along the coast to Anglesey.

At the head of the valley above Betws-y-Coed its character changes again. The wide valley floor is gone and the sides steepen considerably taking on a more alpine character. This is particularly true of Glyn Lledr, often considered to be one of the most attractive valleys in the whole of Wales. Afon Conwy approaches from the east here having plunged through a mile long gorge between the Conwy Falls and Fairy Glen, forming one of the most well known beauty spots in the area.

A good footpath network enables the walker to explore almost every inch of the valley and its hinterland and the walks described in the following pages have been devised to sample as much of its varied character as possible. Thus, while many centre on well known areas, others visit quieter corners where you can expect to be alone. This is particularly true of the eastern side of the valley where the walking is generally more gentle, but the views are often more rewarding.

The climate here is both dryer and milder than that of the adjacent peaks just a few miles away and as such makes a good bad weather alternative to a day in the mountains. The terrain is also suited to those who enjoy the hills but find the higher peaks too strenuous or even too crowded!

The specialist equipment required for the higher peaks will not be needed here but you are advised to wear reasonable quality walking boots and carry warm clothing and a waterproof jacket, especially in the winter months. The higher routes can be exposed and the steeper ground difficult without proper footwear.

It is also recommended that you carry an Ordnance Survey map which will help you locate the starting point of each walk. It will also enable you to identify features from the many excellent views to be enjoyed throughout the valley and if you wander off route, it will get you back to your car!

The recommended maps are the Outdoor Leisure Map 17, Snowdon and Conwy Valley areas and Pathfinder sheet 736. These maps are printed at a scale of 1:25,000 or 2½ inches to one mile and are available almost anywhere locally.

History

In prehistoric times the lower reaches of the Conwy Valley were thickly wooded, inundated by tidal waters and for the most part impenetrable. Evidence for this comes in the almost complete absence of prehistoric remains, in stark contrast to the wealth of such monuments at higher levels.

The earliest remains to be found in the lower valley are probably those of Canovium, the Roman fort at Caerhun (route 6). This was built at an important fording point where the river was at its narrowest and was probably the lowest point at which it could be crossed without the use of a boat. The Romans were not the first to pass this way though, they were merely formalising an existing route which had been in use for many centuries before they arrived. This is evident from the many prehistoric remains which line the route of the old road on its climb to the high pass known as Bwlch-y-Ddeufaen ('pass of the two stones'). Many of these monuments date from as early as the late Stone Age and include the many burial chambers or 'tumulus' as they are often marked on the map. The various standing stones and stone circles are later and date mainly from the Bronze Age, around 1,000 BC.

Another area rich in prehistoric remains is the Great Orme (route 1) at the north end of the valley, an area which undoubtedly attracted prehistoric settlers because of the difficulties presented by penetrating the interior, although the existence of the very early burial chamber at Capel Garmon (route 13) demonstrates that early settlers were active inland on occasions.

Around 500 BC a new group of settlers arrived in Britain, and brought with them the knowledge of a new metal. These were Celtic tribes from central Europe and with them came the period known as the Iron Age. They were a warlike people who were responsible for the many hill forts which exist all over Britain. Notable examples in the Conwy Valley can be seen at Pen-y-gaer above Llanbedr-y-Cennin and near the summit of Conwy Mountain (route 3).

When the Romans arrived, they quickly subdued the tribes of southern Britain but had more difficulty with the Celts who inhabited what is now Wales. Most difficult of all was North Wales and in particular the area around Snowdonia. By AD 45 the Romans were at Chester on what is now the Welsh border, but it took another sixteen years before they penetrated as far as Afon Conwy.

When they did, it was under the general Sutonious Paulinus who crossed Afon Conwy in AD 61 and established an early fort at Caerhun (route 6), before continuing over Bwlch-y-Ddeufaen to carry out his famous slaughter of the Druids on the shores of the Menai Strait. Their victory was short lived however. Queen Boudicea seized the opportunity to revolt and the army was forced to hurry back to the southeast to deal with the uprising. It was not until AD 77 that they returned under Agricola to deal fully with the Ordovices and establish a permanent presence in the area.

The existence of the substantial fort at Segontium (Caernarfon), along with rich mineral deposits in the hills and fine pearls from the river, guaranteed a continued Roman presence at Caerhun throughout this period. A number of Roman roads are known to have existed in the hills to the south and west of Caerhun but their exact line is in doubt.

In the post Roman era the valley became the centre of the newly formed kingdom of Gwynedd. When the Romans left Britain undefended, invaders came to Wales from across the Irish Sea and began to settle. In an attempt to stamp out this colonisation, a powerful Celtic warrior or chieftain called Cunedda Wledig, came from one of the northern British kingdoms in Strathclyde about the year AD 400 and established himself on the little hilltop now known as The

Vardre above Deganwy and at Aberffraw in Anglesey. The struggle against the Irish was continued and finally won by his son Cadwallon, who defeated them in a last battle in Anglesey in AD 470.

Cadwallon's son, Maelgwyn Gwynedd, also ruled from Deganwy and proved to be one of the most famous (or infamous) rulers from this early period. During his rule, which covered the first half of the sixth century, the Irish threat was but a faint memory and he was able to use a period of relative peace and stability to indulge in a hedonistic lifestyle which brought strong condemnation from the church. He is also remembered for his death from a yellow plague, which was seen by many as punishment for his wickedness and is said to have been foretold by the bard Taliesin (see chapter 10).

The following centuries were not so peaceful and Gwynedd's rulers had to fight constantly to retain their kingdom. The Saxon colonisation of southern Britain was swift and by the turn of the seventh century Northumbrian

The Vardre, Deganwy

Saxons had pushed as far west as the River Dee, where in AD 616 they won a decisive battle near Chester. This effectively severed the Celts, who would henceforth be known as the 'Welsh', from their kinsmen in northern England and Cornwall and confine them to the land which we know today as Wales. The Saxons had little success in pushing further west into Wales and in the following century, Offa's Dyke was built to mark the limit of their control.

The Viking raids of the tenth century must have had an impact on the lower reaches of the valley but they left few settlements in North Wales and seemed to have been uninterested in conquering the lands that they raided. This was not true of the Normans who came onto the scene in 1066, the most well known date in our history books. Although their victory was won in a distant corner of Britain, their presence was soon felt in Wales and these new conquerors were not as happy as the Saxons had been to merely contain the Welsh beyond Offa's Dyke. Powerful and ambitious Marcher Lords were established along the border and encouraged to extend their control into Wales.

This brought a time of intense conflict in Wales, not just with the Normans but also between the Welsh themselves. The reason for this was that Wales was still composed of numerous petty kingdoms whose rulers were primarily interested in their own power. As a result the Welsh as a nation were never able to present a united force against Norman rule. Welsh princes even allied themselves with Normans against their own countrymen when it seemed convenient.

It was during this time that Afon Conwy became a defence for the people of Gwynedd. The lands to the east, though more fertile and desirable, were harder to defend and the Normans were able to advance to Afon Clwyd where they established an early castle at Rhuddlan. From here, the push

13

Llanrhychwyn church

west was inevitably along the coast, but the Conwy presented a major obstacle. The fortress at Deganwy, which had been in continuous use for over 600 years, proved inadequate being on the wrong side of the river, however the mountainous heartland of Gwynedd provided defence enough and time and time again the Welsh retreated into the hills leaving Norman armies to starve at Deganwy. Both King John and Henry III suffered humiliation in this way in their wars against Llywelyn ap Iowerth (Llywelyn Fawr or Llywelyn the Great). By this time the Castle had fallen into enemy hands so frequently that Llywelyn ap Gruffydd (grandson of Llywelyn Fawr) finally destroyed it in 1263.

The Conwy Valley has strong links with Llywelyn Fawr. He was born in 1173 at Dolwyddelan Castle in Glyn Lledr, one of the tributary valleys of the upper Conwy and is said to have kept a hunting lodge at Trefriw. He is also associated with the tiny church at Llanrhychwyn (route 9), which he is said to have attended regularly with his wife Princess Joan,

14

the illegitimate daughter of King John. The cistercian abbey at Aberconwy was founded by him and it was here that he died and was buried in 1240. When Edward I had the monks moved to a new site further up the valley at Maenan (route 8) to make way for his new castle and town, they took the stone coffin of their patron with them. The remains of this coffin can be seen today at Llanrwst church (route 9).

When Henry III's son Edward took the crown to become Edward I, he continued his farther's war with Wales but only achieved complete victory after many campaigns and numerous attempts to gain the homage of Llywelyn ap Gruffydd (grandson of Llywelyn the Great, also known as Llywelyn the Last). Edward's final victory came with the death of Llywelyn in a minor skirmish and the capture and execution of his brother Dafydd at Shrewsbury.

When Edward came to Aberconwy, he decided not to rebuild Henry's castle at Deganwy but chose a new site on the west bank of the river. In doing this he was making a political move as much as a strategic one. The last stronghold of Welsh independence was now occupied and controlled by the English. His new town and castle, built on the site of Aberconwy Abbey (route 3), was completed by 1287 and was occupied by English settlers.

Peace with England in the following centuries and the political changes brought about by the Acts of Union in the sixteenth century, brought a measure of prosperity to Wales and a number of prominent families began to acquire large estates. Perhaps the most famous of these in the Conwy Valley are the Wynns of Gwydir. They obtained Gwydir from a descendant of Llywelyn Fawr about 1500 although the present house dates from 1555 and is thought to contain materials from the demolition of Maenan Abbey.

The most famous member of this family is Sir John Wynn (1554-1627) who began numerous local enterprises, such as lead mining around Llyn Geirionydd (route 9) and attempts to make the river navigable as far as Llanrwst. He also had an active political career and travelled far and wide.

The need for such travel and for the transport of goods during this time highlighted the poor condition of the road system nationally and particularly in the difficult terrain of North Wales. In the Conwy Valley, communications were still based on the ancient crossing at Caerhun, where the Tal-y-Cafn ferry operated. A second ferry crossed the mouth of the river between Deganwy and Conwy. A number of ancient drovers roads were also in use but would have been too poor for use by wheeled vehicles.

With the development of the postal service in the sixteenth century came the need to reach Ireland on a regular basis. The established port for the dispatch of the mail was Holyhead, so the road through North Wales became of major importance. The crossing of the Conwy was one of the main obstacles en-route from Chester to Holyhead and was achieved by means of the two ferries already mentioned. Two roads approached these ferries. The older Tal-y-Cafn route followed the approximate line of the old Roman road from Chester to Caernarfon and was known as the 'Old Chester Road'. This continued over Bwlch-y-Ddeufaen to reach Anglesey by the Lafan Sands. The other route was known as the 'Great Irish Road' and came via Denbigh to what is now Glan Conwy Corner. From there travellers made use of an ancient causeway known as 'Sarn y Mynach', which crossed the marshes of Afon Ganol to approach the Conwy ferry at Deganwy.

The river crossing was not the end of the problems however. Before the nineteenth century there was no road around the coast as there is today. This route was guarded by the precipitous headlands of Penmaenbach and Penmaenmawr, so the traveller had a choice depending on

The Sychnant Pass

the state of the tide. If this was favourable, a shorter route along the sands to Llanfairfechan could be taken but at high tide a detour inland using the Sychnant Pass was the only option. This however, still left a difficult and dangerous traverse of Penmaenmawr, a route almost impossible by coach. In fact coaches were almost nonexistent on our roads until the turn of the eighteenth century and it was at this time that a greater interest in road improvement began.

By this time Conwy had developed a considerable trade catering for travellers using the 'Great Irish Road'. After a ferry crossing, travellers would require refreshment and accommodation to prepare for the difficult traverse of Penmaenmawr and the Lafan Sands. Such frequent use of the ferry should have produced an efficient service but this seems not to have been the case. The Conwy ferry in particular is reported to have been expensive, infrequent and dangerous and a number of fatalities are recorded. Because of this and the unacceptable delays which became a regular feature of the ferry, an alternative route became a major concern.

The increasing use of coaches in the mid to late 1700s made the problem even worse and in the 1770s an alternative route was found. This took a line further south through Shrewsbury and Llangollen missing out Chester and Denbigh. From Llangollen it followed a similar line to the present A5 to Pentrefoelas, then turned northwards through the village of Nebo. This avoided the steep gorge near the Conwy Falls and instead made use of a long descent to Llanrwst where a crossing of the Conwy was made by Pont Fawr—the 'large' or 'great bridge' (see route 9). From here the road along the river's west bank was followed either to Conwy or over Bwlch-y-Ddeufaen.

This new route is said to have been built at the instigation of a Shrewsbury inn keeper by the name of Robert Lawrence. When the road was complete he immediately began a London to Holyhead coach service.

Edward I's castle and Thomas Telford's bridge at Conwy

Llanrwst was also quick to recognise this new found prosperity. Inns and hotels were built to cater for travellers using the new coach road, however its prosperity was to last only until the end of the century. The route beyond Conwy was still a problem and a planned Turnpike Road over Bwlch-y-Ddeufaen was never constructed. The answer came when Lord Penrhyn built a new road through Nant Francon to link the mines near Ty Hyll (the 'Ugly House' on what is now the A5 west of Betws-y-Coed) with the port at Bangor. In 1803, the short section between Ty Hyll and Pentrefoelas was added by the Capel Curig Turnpike Trust, to provide a complete inland road avoiding all the previous problems of the coastal route via Conwy.

The line of this link road is now no more than a footpath where it passes through the gorge below the A5 (see routes 14 and 15). It became redundant just 12 years after completion, when in 1815 Thomas Telford improved the whole route from London to Holyhead and built his graceful suspension bridge across the Menai Strait in 1819, thus avoiding a crossing of the Lafan Sands.

This new inland route led to the growth and prosperity of Betws-y-Coed during the nineteenth century. Originally a posting-point on the Irish mail route, it developed as a popular tourist destination after being 'discovered' by the Victorians. The romantic location appealed to them and they came here in large numbers now that new roads made travel easier. It was this that enabled it to survive when Thomas Telford improved the coast road through Conwy and Llanfairfechan, incorporating his famous bridge across the estuary in 1826. This diverted the mail route away from Betws-y-Coed and back to the coast, however its new found popularity as a tourist destination kept the visitors coming.

This was speeded up by the development of the railways in the mid 1800s, although initially they were a threat to the village's prosperity. The new Chester to Holyhead line followed the coastal route and bridged the river at Conwy, where Robert Stephenson built his bridge close to that of Telford's. This brought the coastal areas around Llandudno and Colwyn Bay within easy reach of many more tourists and allowed them to develop as popular resorts throughout the late nineteenth and early twentieth centuries. Betws-y-Coed would have remained isolated but a branch line was constructed linking it to the main line at Llandudno Junction. This made the entire valley and in particular Betws-y-Coed easily accessible to the tourist and tourism continues to be its main concern today.

Elsewhere things were developing fast. The Mostyn family were busy turning an area of waste and common on an isolated headland into one of the most fashionable resorts of the Victorian period—Llandudno. The new rail line along the coast brought huge numbers of tourists to Llandudno from the high population areas of Liverpool and Manchester. The same can be said of Colwyn Bay and Rhos-on-Sea, although these resorts never attained Llandudno's popularity with the wealthy.

The Conwy Valley has seen many changes over its long and often troubled history but one continuing theme has been its barrier to communications and the way in which this has been dealt with has had a great impact on the settlement and fortunes of the valley. Slight changes in these events would have produced very different results. The eventual triumph of the coastal route for both road and rail has led to the heaviest development in those areas, likewise the failure of a once popular route, such as that over Bwlch-y-Ddeufaen, or Lawrence's road through Nebo, has spared those areas the ravages of modern development. For this the walker can be glad, for away from the coastal fringe the valley is, for the most part, unspoilt and can rightly claim to be one of North Wales' most beautiful areas.

Map of the Conwy Valley and the location of the walks

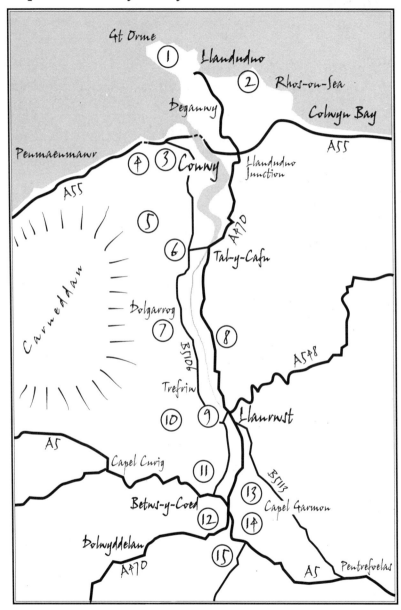

Glossary of Welsh names

Aber	*river mouth*	Dyffryn	*valley*
Abaty	*abbey*	Eglwys	*church*
Afon	*river*	Eryri	*highland*
Bach	*little*	Esgair	*ridge*
Bryn	*hill, eminence*	Fach	*small*
Cae	*field, enclosure*	Faes	*meadow*
Caer	*fort*	Fawr	*large*
Canol	*middle*	Felin	*mill*
Capel	*chapel*	Ffordd	*road*
Carn, Carnedd	*heap of stones*	Ffynnon	*well or fountain*
Carreg	*crag or stone*	Foel	*bare hill*
Castell	*castle or fortress*	Gaer	*camp*
Cefn	*ridge*	Galt	*slope*
Clogwyn	*cliff*	Garn	*an eminence*
Clwyd	*gate*	Glas	*blue-green*
Coch	*red*	Glyn	*deep valley*
Coed	*wood*	Goch	*red*
Cors	*bog or swamp*	Gors	*swamp*
Craig	*crag*	Grach	*scabby*
Crib	*jagged ridge*	Groes	*cross*
Croes	*cross*	Gwern	*alder coppice*
Cwm	*coombe*	Gwyn	*white*
Dinas	*city, fortress*	Hafod	*summer dwelling*
Ddu	*black*	Hen	*old*

22

Isaf	*lower*	Rhos	*moorland*
Llan	*church*	Rhyd	*ford*
Llyn	*lake*	Sarn	*causeway*
Llys	*hall or court*	Tomen	*mound*
Lon	*lane*	Traeth	*beach, sandy shore*
Maen	*stone*	Tref	*town*
Maes	*field or meadow*	Trwyn	*peninsula*
Mawr	*large*	Twll	*cavern*
Moel	*rounded hill*	Twr	*tower*
Mor	*sea*	Ty	*house*
Morfa	*flat seashore, sea fen*	Tyddyn	*farmstead*
Mynach	*monk*	Uchaf	*upper*
Mynydd	*mountain*	Waun	*moorland*
Newydd	*new*	Wen	*white*
Ogof	*cave*	Wern	*alder swamp*
Pant	*hollow*	Y, Yr	*the*
Parc	*park*	Yn	*in*
Pen	*head or point*	Ynys	*island*
Penrhyn	*promontory*		
Pentre	*village*		
Pistyll	*waterfall*		
Plas	*house*		
Pont	*bridge*		
Porth	*port*		
Pwll	*pool*		

1. The Great Orme

Distance: 5 *miles*

Start: Begin the walk at the northern end of The Parade in Llandudno. There is a car park at the cable car station just before the start of the toll road around the Great Orme (Marine Drive). Alternatively, park in Llandudno and follow the signs to the cable car station.
Grid ref. 782 828 (Ordnance Survey Pathfinder 736).

The Route

1. If you are starting from Llandudno, walk along North Parade and just before the Grand Hotel turn sharp left onto a paved footpath. This quickly rises to give a fine view out over Llandudno Bay to the Little Orme with the hills and mountains of Snowdonia beyond. Follow the path to the cable car station in Happy Valley.

From the little car park, walk up the road which climbs steeply to the ski slope and toboggan run. At the top of the hill turn right and follow a well worn footpath with the ski slope to your left. At the top of the rise turn right and walk over the grass for a few yards to a fine viewpoint overlooking Llandudno Bay.

This is one of the finest viewpoints in the area giving a grand panorama over much of the town, with Llandudno Bay curving eastwards to the Little Orme. Beyond lie the resorts of Colwyn Bay and Rhyl with the Clwydian Hills on the skyline. In very clear conditions the tip of the Wirral and the Lancashire coast can occasionally be seen.

To the south beyond Llandudno, the little hill known as The Vardre (site of the ancient court of the princes of Gwynedd) stands guard over the mouth of Afon Conwy, with Conwy Mountain and the headlands of Penmaenbach and Penmaenmawr out to the west. Beyond these foothills, the higher tops of the Carneddau rise to well over 3,000 feet culminating in Carnedd Llywelyn, Wales' second highest summit.

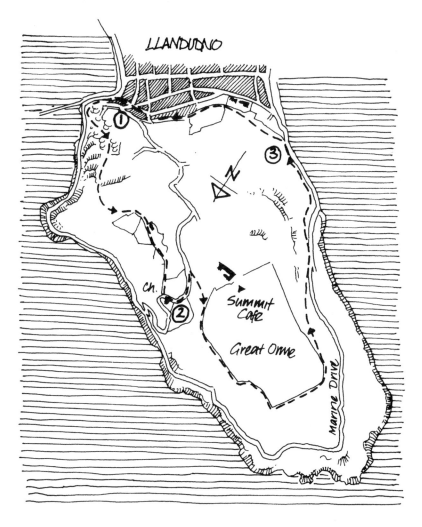

The present form of Llandudno owes its existence to the Mostyn family who obtained the land on which it is now built by an Act of Parliament in 1843. This enabled them to enclose what was then a large area of open common land. Prior to this, Llandudno had been confined to the sloping ground on the southern side of the Great Orme, close to where the tramway now runs up to the summit of the Great Orme. Copper mining had sustained it throughout the previous century and was still its main activity when the Mostyns bought the adjacent common. Fortunately for them, the mines were forced to close in the 1860s because of extensive flooding.

From the start, the Mostyns seemed to have known exactly what they were doing. The town was carefully planned and individual plots sold for lease in 1849 subject to strict conditions. Shortly afterwards, a branch line was constructed providing a link with the cities of Liverpool, Chester and Manchester at a time when the railways were bringing totally new ideas and attitudes towards travel. By the close of the century Llandudno was the most fashionable resort in North Wales.

Rejoin the path at a four fingered sign taking the signed route to "St Tudno's Church". This curves leftwards over the rounded hillside of Mynydd Isaf and heads towards the small hill farm of Penmynydd Isa. Turn right at the edge of fields on the right and walk towards the farm turning right again just before the house onto an enclosed footpath, signposted "St Tudno's Church". Follow this path past Ffynnon Powl to the church, situated on a green terrace overlooking the sea.

2. Turn left (or right if coming out of the church gate) up the lane and about 300 yards past the cemetery look for a track on the right which contours the hillside. It is possible to make a short detour to the summit from here. If you do, return to this track to continue the walk.

On either side of the track are traces of Medieval field systems along with the outlines of two groups of long huts higher up the slope near the summit. The cultivation ridges can still be seen and reach down to the edge of the cemetery.

The exact date of these field systems is not known, although there is known to have been activity and settlement on the Great Orme from prehistoric times. Of particular note is the Neolithic burial chamber known as Lletty'r Filiast and the Bronze Age mines which are open to the public. This site has proved to be one of the most important examples of Bronze Age mining in the country. Visitors can embark on a guided tour of the workings and see how, with simple tools and the technique of 'firesetting'—the weakening

Llandudno from the Great Orme

of the rock by the lighting of fires and breaking with large hammer-stones, the valuable ore was extracted.

Follow the track with a high stone wall on your left for almost one mile passing Ffynnon Rufeinig. Eventually the wall makes a sharp turn to the left and the track continues straight ahead to one of the car parks on the Marine Drive. Turn left here, continue beside the wall and at the top of the rise there is a ruined stone cairn with a fine view out over Conwy Bay towards Anglesey.

A number of 'limestone pavements' can be seen in this area. These features are normally associated with the Pennine areas of Yorkshire and occur in exposed locations where the soil is thin, allowing rainwater to dissolve the rock into these strange patterns.

Stay beside the wall until a well worn path bears right and drops diagonally down the steep hillside to the road. Turn left along the road and after about 200 yards, just beyond a turning on the right, bear left onto a track signposted "To Grey Gables". After a few hundred yards, the track splits—take the right-hand fork and follow the well worn footpath with a wall on the right at first, then a fence along the steep hillside overlooking Conwy Sands.

3. The path eventually drops to the road with a lodge house on the right. Turn left up a tarmac road which leads onto a footpath higher up. This zig-zags up the hillside before contouring the steeper ground. There is a fine view over the town from this path which eventually passes through a small park to join a road. Follow the road down the hill and make your way through the streets back to your starting point. If you began the walk at the foot of the cable car station, refer to the first part of point 1.

2. The Little Orme

Distance: *4¾ miles*

Start: Drive east along The Parade in Llandudno for about one mile and turn right into Nant y Gamar Road. Follow the road steeply uphill to a small car park on the edge of common land.
Grid ref. 802 813 (Ordnance Survey Pathfinder 736).

The Route

1. From the parking area return to the road and turn right following what has now become a gravel access road with fields on the left. At the end of the fields, bear half-left onto a prominent footpath indicated by a waymark on a nearby post (ignore a footpath immediately on the left here). Follow the obvious footpath through gorse and bracken, veering to the right after about 600 yards.

As you approach the corner of the field with a house to the left and wall enclosed woods on the right, look for a metal kissing gate which leads onto an enclosed footpath. At the end of the path a second kissing gate leads into an open wood. Ignore a footpath which drops to the right, instead keep straight ahead, veering left slightly. At the far side of the wood, a kissing gate leads out of the trees and onto a path with gardens on the right. Follow the path to a gate which takes you via a short enclosed footpath to the road in Penrhynside. Turn left along the road and at a T junction turn left again. Walk through the village.

Leave the houses behind and walk down to a T junction. Cross the road here and turn right past the "Llandudno Welcomes You" sign, then keep left along the footpath following the busy main road. After about 300 yards look for a signed footpath on the right which carries the North Wales Path (NWP) waymark. This path leads diagonally-right up the bank at first before curving left with grazing fields on the right. At the top of the rise, a post carrying the NWP waymark confirms that you are on the right path.

For a fine panorama of the bays to the east and west, a short detour can be made from here to the summit of the Little Orme. Follow the path to the left, steeply at first, then bear right over rocks to the triangulation pillar on the summit. Return to this point to continue the walk.

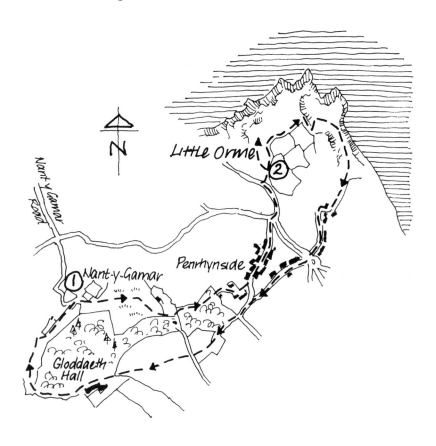

The wide sweep of Llandudno Bay and the rounded mass of the Great Orme dominate the view from this exposed summit. Inland, rolling limestone hills contrast with the harder volcanic rocks of Snowdonia which rise to over 3,000 feet, with the summit of Carnedd Llywelyn being Wales' second highest mountain at 3,485 feet. Out to the west, the dramatic headlands at Penmaenmawr and Llanfairfechan lead the eye along the coast to Anglesey. Eastwards, the resorts of Rhos-on-Sea, Colwyn Bay, Abergele and Rhyl line the coast, with the Clwydian Hills on the skyline. The tip of the Wirral and the Lancashire coast can be seen in very clear conditions.

2. Continue along the obvious footpath keeping fields to the right. After a kissing gate keep right and pass through an area of gorse bushes and sheep tracks. Waymarker posts keep you on the right path until you arrive abruptly at the edge of quarry workings. Turn right along the edge of the quarry face (take care!) until a waymarker (NWP) directs you left. Descend diagonally to a large flat grassed area at the foot of the quarry face. Walk across the grass to the remains of winding gear, turn right, go through a metal kissing gate and walk down one of the old inclines. At the bottom of the slope turn right onto a white gravel track and follow this, making detours around recent landslips which have now been fenced off for safety reasons. Stay on the track ignoring the North Wales Path which bears left down steps into a housing estate.

At the end of the quarry area, go through a metal kissing gate on the right and follow an access road between houses. Continue to the main road. Turn left down the hill and at the roundabout cross the road (turn right) and walk down Penrhyn Old Road. Beyond Penrhyn Old Hall continue along a rough track and at Derwen Lane turn left. At the first bend take the signed footpath on the right. This footpath leads into woods and the path splits—keep left here and follow

Llandudno Bay and the Great Orme

the obvious path through the trees. Where the path leaves the woods, cross a farm track and enter the large field opposite. Walk directly through the field following a line of posts, then aim for an iron kissing gate in the top corner of the field. Follow the path beside Gloddaeth Hall to join an access track beyond a stile. Turn right along the track and after about 60 yards bear half-right onto a path which follows the edge of woods on the right. Immediately after an iron kissing gate the path splits—take the right-hand fork and at a waymarker bear right again. This path takes you to the top of the hill overlooking Llandudno.

There is a grand view from here taking in much of Llandudno, the Great Orme, Anglesey and the headland at Penmaenmawr. Inland, Conwy Castle can just be seen guarding the waters of Afon Conwy, with the Conwy Valley and the mountains of Snowdonia behind.

Nearer at hand is the distinctive hilltop known as The Vardre where the princes of Gwynedd built their courts and fortresses for over 700 years, from the time of King Maelgwyn in the sixth century, to Llywelyn the Last, a contemporary of Edward I. Even the English built here. The last castle, whose remains can still be seen, was built by Henry III and destroyed by Llywelyn ap Gruffydd (Llywelyn the Last) in 1263.

The strategic role of the Conwy Valley in defending the kingdom of Gwynedd was one of the reasons which led Edward I to choose Conwy as the site for his new castle in 1283 and not The Vardre as his farther, Henry III had done. Throughout the centuries of their conflict with the English, the cultivated lands around Deganwy were heavily populated by the Welsh but when trouble showed itself, usually in the form of Norman armies advancing along the coast from the east, they would cross the Conwy and disappear into the mountains. This technique was used with success against both King John and Henry III, who found themselves isolated here and, facing starvation were forced to retreat.

At the top of the slope, walk a few yards to the corner of a small walled field, then keep straight ahead between walls. Join the access track to a house on the left, turn right and follow the track back to the car park.

3. Conwy Mountain

Distance: 6½ miles

Start: Begin the walk at the long stay car park situated on the B5106 just outside of the town walls.
Grid ref. 782 773 (Ordnance Survey Outdoor Leisure Map 17).

The Route

1. From the car park walk through the underpass and bear left up steps to enter the town through Porth-y-Felin or 'Mill Gate'. This was one of the three original gates in the town walls and gave access to the town's mill by Afon Gyffin, situated approximately where the car park is today. Turn right along Rose Hill Street and walk towards the castle.

The castle and town walls were built by Edward I as a complete unit between 1283 and 1287 following his conquest of Wales and the defeat of Prince Llywelyn and his brother Dafydd. This was one of a chain of castles which he built around the coast of North Wales to hold his newly conquered lands in subjection.

The strategic importance of the crossing of the Conwy had been realised over 1,000 years earlier by the Romans who built a fort (Canovium) seven miles upstream at Caerhun where their road crossed the river. Centuries later King Maelgwyn, who founded the kingdom of Gwynedd in the sixth century, built a fortress at Deganwy on a hilltop now known as The Vardre for this same purpose. In Maelgwyn's day, the main threat to Gwynedd came from across the Irish Sea, but by the time of Llywelyn Fawr, invaders came from the east—first Saxons then Norman Marcher Lords. The castle at Deganwy fell into enemy hands too many times to be of any real use and was finally destroyed by the sons of Llywelyn the Great after his death in 1240. The ruins which can be seen at Deganwy today are the remains of a later castle built by Henry III

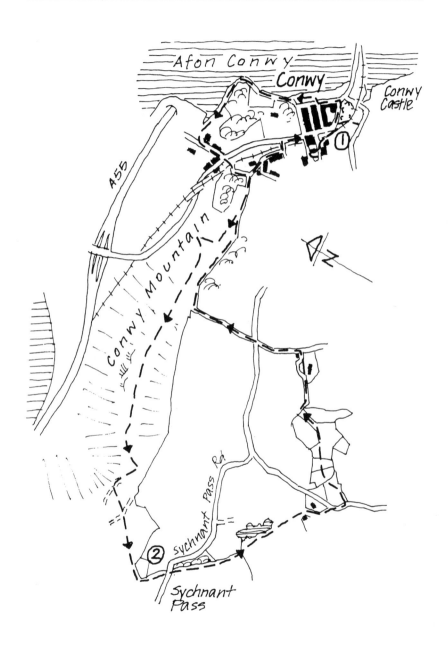

between 1245-54. This was destroyed by Llywelyn ap Gruffydd in 1263 after a long siege and never rebuilt.

When the victorious Edward I arrived here in 1283, he made the bold decision not to rebuild Henry's castle at Deganwy, but to establish a new castle and town on the western bank of the river in what had been the heartland of the kingdom of Gwynedd. The site he chose was occupied at the time by Aberconwy Abbey and one of Llywelyn's courts. The monks were moved out and given land eight miles up river at Maenan and their abbey pulled down. The present parish church incorporates the foundations of this building but nothing else remains. Part of Llywelyn's court was incorporated into the town walls.

During the Middle Ages, Conwy was used increasingly as a port for Ireland; a function which brought Richard II here in 1399. Richard was returning from Ireland to confront the rebellion of Henry Bolingbroke, Duke of Lancaster, who was then stationed at Chester. He was enticed from the safety of Conwy Castle and into an ambush by the Earl of Northumberland who had promised him safe conduct to Flint Castle to hold talks with Henry. The ambush took place at Penmaenrhos near Old Colwyn and after seizing the throne to become Henry IV, Bolingbroke is believed to have brought about Richard's death.

Conwy saw action early in the following century when rebels under Owain Glyndwr took the castle and burnt part of the town in 1401, but by the time of the Civil War, the castle and town walls had begun to crumble and their days of conflict seemed to be over. This was not to be the case for the Royalist John Williams, Archbishop of York who was a native of Conwy, returned and carried out repairs on the castle and town walls. He then held Conwy for the Crown until a quarrel with one of the king's commanders led to him joining the Parliamentary army. In 1646 Conwy surrendered and orders were given to render its walls and castle unusable again. Although there was a certain amount of damage, the promised destruction seems not to have happened.

Turn left into Castle Street immediately after The Bridge (*Y Bont*) public house and walk down to Aberconwy House on the left (National Trust shop).

This is the oldest house in the town and dates from the thirteenth century. It is typical of the kind of dwelling built during the Middle Ages, although the majority would have been built entirely of timber. The stone and timber construction of Aberconwy House suggest that it may have been built by a wealthy merchant and probably explains why this example has survived so well.

Turn right here and walk out of the walls through Porth Isaf (Lower Gate) and onto the sea front. Turn left along the front passing the smallest house in Wales and exit through the walls again. After about 20 yards the road forks and a finger post indicates the North Wales Path which bears right

On Conwy Mountain

here. This is Marine Walk and passes between two black and white houses—'Shore Cottage' and 'Glan yr Arfon'. Follow Marine Walk with views across the river to Deganwy and The Vardre, site of the ancient castle of Maelgwyn Gwynedd.

At the end of Marine Walk turn left along the road and at the main road cross over. A short track directly opposite leads to a footbridge over the railway. Beyond this, continue along the road and at the T junction turn right up Mountain Road, indicated by the North Wales Path sign. At the top of the rise bear right (North Wales Path sign) and pass a terrace of stone cottages on the right. After a few yards, a ladder style leads onto the open moor. The path is steep for some distance now and rises through the heather and gorse to a col and a junction of paths. Turn right here and walk to a small summit with a grand view over the Conwy estuary to the Great Orme.

From here turn around and instead of returning to the col, bear right following a path which keeps just to the right of the main ridge. Continue on this route until you reach the highest point—a series of rocky summits. From here take the most obvious path which continues in the direction of the Sychnant Pass (a stone farm surrounded by green fields is directly ahead now). Lower down, the path bends left and about 100 yards before a stone wall with fields beyond, turn right onto a narrow contouring path. This is not a very broad path, but within a 100 yards or so you will pass a squat wooden post carrying the waymark of the North Wales Path, if you are in the right location. Soon you will come to the edge of the steep slopes overlooking the sea with quarry workings to the right; bear left here. Again you will see waymarked posts at frequent intervals. Where the path forks, keep right and at the next junction go straight ahead. At the bottom of the slope cross a farm access track (farm to the right), make a short rise then drop to join the track which you should now follow to the road. This is the summit of the Sychnant Pass.

2. Cross the road and go through the metal gate directly opposite. The footpath now keeps close to a wall on the left. A little further on, an old iron ladder stile leads over the wall and the path passes close to a small marshy lake on the left. At a T junction turn right and follow the track as it curves leftwards past a farm on the right. Continue along the track to the road.

Turn right and walk along the road for about 120 yards. Just before a house (Bwythyn) turn left through an iron kissing gate and follow an enclosed footpath into fields. Bear half-left through the first field to a gate in the hedge then follow a line of gates in the following fields. Keep to the left of a wood and look for a kissing gate in the top right-hand corner of the field among the trees. Turn right along the road and where this bears left (after about 300 yards) go through a pair of large stone pillars with Oakwood Park Hall to the right. Walk straight across the grassed area in front of the hall and exit through a pair of identical pillars. Keep right here and walk down the driveway to a quiet lane. Turn left along the lane and continue to Sychnant Pass Road.

Turn right, then immediately left onto a bridleway. Follow this track over a stream and rise to a gate which leads onto the open hillside again. Turn right here following a good path and at a fork bear right keeping beside the wall. Lower down go through a metal gate and join Mountain Road again. Follow this road down the hill and up a slight rise to a T junction. Turn left and follow the road which eventually bends left over the railway to join the main road at a T junction. Turn right now and enter the town walls through the gate known as the "Bangor Arch".

This gateway is not one of the original gates to the town but was sympathetically created from one of the towers by Thomas Telford, when he built his graceful suspension bridge across the estuary, as part of his improvements to the coast road in the 1820s.

39

A view of Conwy Castle and town from the walls

Immediately after the gate, turn left and take the steps up onto the Town Walls. Turn left along the walls and walk up to the tower at the highest point of the defences. A wooden footbridge and steps allow you to reach the top of the tower.

This is the highest tower in the walls and gives a fine view of the entire town and castle. Its position is unique in being forward of the wall line, thus allowing defenders a clear view along the outside of the wall. The open back to each tower is not the result of decay, but part of the original design. The gaps were crossed by means of removable wooden footbridges which enabled each section of the wall-walk to be isolated if the walls were breached.

Keep right along the wall-walk to the next tower known as Porth Uchaf—the 'Upper Gate'.

This is one of the town's three original gates and the only one with a landward approach. It was originally defended by a drawbridge and portcullis and contained guardrooms and porter's chamber. These would have been wooden buildings built against the walls.

The walls are not accessible beyond here, so descend the steps and turn right into Rosemary Lane. Immediately beyond St Michael's Hall, turn right onto a paved footpath which brings you beside the walls again.

The three windows which can be seen in the wall here belong to an earlier building known as 'Llywelyn's Court'. This was incorporated into the walls rather than demolished and may have been the venue for peace talks between Edward I and Llywelyn ap Gruffydd in 1277.

Continue down steps and keep right to pass out of the walls by a large archway.

To the left now you will see the breach in the walls made by Stephenson's railway (1847) and a little further on, one of the most unique features of the entire defences—12 latrines corbelled out from the walls. They are thought to have been built for the use of Clerks of the King's Wardrobe and the office of Master of the King's Works (at that time Master James of St George, who was responsible for the design of all Edward's Welsh castles). These offices would have been built of wood against the walls.

Something else to bear in mind when considering the positioning of the latrines and the apparent weakness caused by the windows of Llywelyn's Court is that this section of wall originally overlooked a small tidal inlet (Afon Gyffin) which also powered the mill. This has since been filled in and is now the site of the car park.

Return to the car park at Point 1.

41

4. Capelulo

Distance: *6¼ miles*

Start: There is parking available for a number of cars at the top of the Sychnant Pass. *Grid ref. 750 770.* If this is full there is parking available on the Conwy side of the pass *Grid ref. 756 767 (Ordnance Survey Outdoor Leisure Map 17).*

The Route

1. From the car park at the top of the pass, go through the large metal gate between stone pillars on the south side of the road. Follow a good footpath with woods on the left for about 200 yards before turning sharp right as indicated by the North Wales Path (NWP) sign. Rise gently up the hillside and where the path levels, turn left onto a broad grassy track (NWP). Where the path forks a little further on keep right, then turn right at the next junction (NWP). At a junction of paths below power cables keep directly ahead; a waymark (NWP) about 100 yards further on confirms that you are on the right route. Follow this path for almost ½ mile.

A ladder stile leads over the wall and a track curves in from the left. Climb over the stile and follow the track straight ahead. Beyond a white farmhouse down to the right, the track curves leftwards then forks; keep right here (NWP) and walk beside a stone wall on the right. Where the path forks again and the wall curves away to the right, keep straight ahead (really you are taking the left fork) and continue to a ruined stone farm (ignore a left fork just before this). Turn right (NWP) and follow the wall bearing half-left at the corner to a footbridge over a stream.

2. Beyond the stream a good footpath heads towards a farm (Ty'n-y-ffrith). Just before the farm there is a fork in the path—the North Wales Path bears left, but our way lies to the right.

A ladder stile leads over the wall and the footpath bears half-left to a col. At a junction of unmade roads, join the access road to Ty'n-y-ffrith and bear left down the hill. As you begin to descend, a path can be seen on the right which will take you to the summit of Foel Lus for those who wish to make the detour. Return to this point to continue the walk.

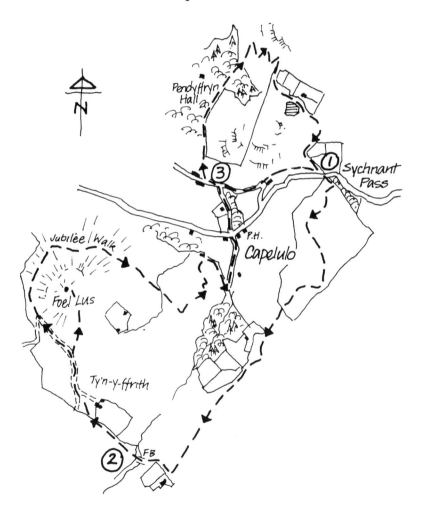

Continue down the road to a sharp left-hand bend. Turn right here off the road and walk between two large stone pillars which mark the beginning of a contouring path.

This path is known as Jubilee Walk and was opened in 1888 to commemorate Queen Victoria's Jubilee the previous year. It follows the 800 foot contour and gives dramatic views into the valley of Penmaenmawr and Dwygyfylchi, as well as across the bay to the Great Orme and Penmon Point on Anglesey.

This sheltered valley is enclosed by the two great headlands of Penmaenbach and Penmaenmawr which caused travellers so much trouble in the days before the coast road was built. During the seventeenth and eighteenth centuries, the route from Chester to Holyhead on Anglesey was known as the 'Great Irish Road' and came to Conwy via Denbigh—this however, was its most notorious section. Coaches were often taken along the beach at low tide while passengers proceeded on foot or horseback over the Sychnant Pass and the precarious route over Penmaenmawr. There was then a dangerous crossing of the Lafan Sands to the ferry at Beaumaris.

Jubilee Walk ends on the far side of Foel Lus overlooking Capelulo and the Sychnant Pass (there is also a bench and power cables overhead here). Continue straight ahead and take the first path on the left which drops diagonally down the hillside to a stream. Cross the stream and ignoring the footpath on the left, keep straight ahead up the bank. Take a direct line now to join a broad grass track at a T junction. Turn left and follow the track down the hillside passing a small cottage on the left (ignore signed footpaths on the left). Beyond the cottage, the track enters woods and drops to a gate. Go through the gate and turn sharp left to follow Fairy Glen Road into Capelulo.

Although Capelulo is an ancient settlement, the village in its present form came into being when the Sychnant Pass road was opened in 1772. This road linked Conwy to Holyhead and avoided the long and strenuous climb to Bwlch-y-Ddeufaen above Rowen, or a dangerous crossing of the sands below the headland of Penmaenbach. For a while it formed part of the Irish mail road which came via Denbigh and the ferry at Conwy. Three inns were opened to provide lodgings and refreshment for those ascending or descending the pass.

This trade came to a sudden end in 1825 when Thomas Telford built a bridge at Conwy and a new road along the coast (the old A55). Capelulo returned to its former seclusion until the 1870s when Victorian tourists discovered the area and came to admire its dramatic scenery. Excursions from the nearby growing resort of Llandudno were popular around the turn of the century.

Jubilee Walk

There are two pubs here—the Fairy Glen Hotel and Y Dwygyfylchi. Between the pubs on the opposite side of the road there is an enclosed footpath; follow this path to a second road. For a shorter round turn right here, walk up the lane and at the bend, take the rising footpath straight ahead up the valley back to the car park (½ mile).

3. Alternatively, for a longer finish incorporating the woods of Pendyffryn Hall (1¼ miles), turn left and walk down the lane to a bridge over the stream on the right. Cross the bridge turning right immediately and walk in front of stone cottages. At the end of the terrace take a signed footpath on the left which passes behind the houses, then bears right up steps into the woods. Follow a contouring path through the trees until the path splits and the hall is visible to the left. Bear right here (arrow) and follow a zig-zag path to the top edge of the woods before continuing to contour with a wall to your right. Further on, the path makes a short drop to join a track coming up from Pendyffryn Hall. Turn right here and follow the path as it continues to rise.

Once out of the trees, continue on the obvious path ignoring a footpath on the right which cuts directly up the hillside. A little further on, the path narrows and there is a fork; keep right here and zig-zag up the hillside. At the top of the slope turn right at a T junction and follow a good footpath beside a wall enclosed field on the left. At the end of the wall bear left to a small lake keeping to the left of the water to join a broad path which runs beside the wall. Bear right onto a farm access road and follow this to a finger post carrying the North Wales Path signs. Turn right here, rise over a bank and drop to join the track again, which you should now follow back to the Sychnant Pass.

5. Rowen

Distance: *3¾ miles*

Start: From Ty'n-y-groes on the B5106 take the signed lane west to Rowen. This pretty village sits at the foot of the eastern Carneddau close to the old Roman road over the hills to Caernarfon. Cars can be parked at a number of locations in the village. Begin the walk at the Ty Gwyn Hotel.
Grid ref. 758 720 (Ordnance Survey Outdoor Leisure Map 17).

The Route

1. From the Ty Gwyn Hotel, walk up the lane through the village and bear right at a fork (as indicated by the Youth Hostel sign). This lane takes you out of Rowen and steepens considerably on its approach to the Youth Hostel. Follow the lane for about ¾ mile.

This lane follows the line of the old Roman road which led over the hills to Abergwyngregyn and then along the coast to the fort at Segontium (Caernarfon). The Romans were not the first to travel this way though, a road over these hills had been in common use for centuries before they arrived. Evidence for this exists in the many prehistoric remains to be seen higher up the lane beyond the Youth Hostel and on the moors near the summit of the pass at Bwlch-y-Ddeufaen ('pass of the two stones').

The use of this route continued throughout the Middle Ages and only fell into disuse with the building of new coach roads during the eighteenth century.

After a series of bends the angle eases and the lane straightens. About 200 yards before the Youth Hostel, look to the right and locate a well hidden metal gate. Go through the gate and bear left up the bank to rise steeply along the left-hand field edge. Cross the remains of an old stone wall and look back for a grand view of the Conwy Valley and the eastern Carneddau. From this point, the right of way bears half-right through the centre of the field.

2. At the top of the field, where the slope becomes more gentle, there is a large well built stone wall and if you have taken the correct route through the field there will be a ladder stile marking the right of way. Beyond the stile keep right and after the ruins of a second stone wall, bear right again, passing the little hill fort of Caer Bach on your left.

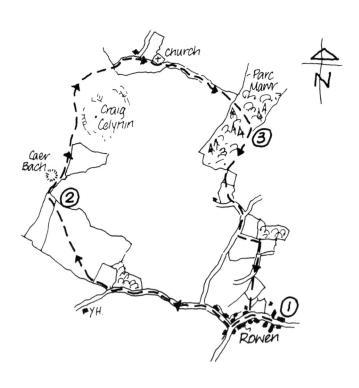

This hill fort, tiny by comparison with the nearby fortifications on Pen-y-gaer, is little more than 80m in diameter but commands a fine panorama of the Conwy valley. There is little for the untrained eye to see except for a ditch on the south and east sides. The remains of a rectangular hut built across the ditch are much later, possibly a 'hafod' or summer hut from the late Middle Ages.

Immediately after Caer Bach there is a stone sheep pen; keep to the left of this and follow a more ruined stone wall with a small rocky hilltop (Craig Celynin) directly ahead.

As you approach Craig Celynin the faint remains of a track become visible; follow this track as it bypasses the hill on its left-hand side, then curves right towards a farm (Garnedd-wen). Just before the farm go through a large gate and bear right almost immediately where the track forks. Follow the track to the tiny church of St Celynin which lies to the left of the path after about 200 yards.

The main fabric of this fascinating little church dates from the fourteenth century—an estimate you will likely agree with once you have looked inside. The interior is very plain and simple but conveys a great sense of age and history. The nave is the oldest part with the chancel being added in the following century. Several later additions were demolished in the 1800s and the building has remained unaltered ever since. Probably the biggest surprise is that the visitor can so freely enter and look around the building, yet there is no sign of vandalism. Renovation work was carried out in 1987 by Gerald Speechley, an event commemorated by a small plaque located inside the church.

Outside the church are a number of informally arranged gravestones dating from the early 1700s and in the corner of the yard is Ffynnon Celynin, a tiny wall enclosed well, reputed to be an ancient holy well associated with St Celynin, which probably predates the church.

The remote location of the church can be explained by the fact that during the Middle Ages, numerous ancient roads made their way over the northern spurs of these hills because of the inaccessibility of the coastal route. In earlier centuries an inn existed here for the refreshment of travellers. Its remains lie near to the churchyard gate.

Turn left out of the church gate and follow the wall enclosed bridleway down to the woods of Parc Mawr. Enter the trees at a gate and descend steeply into the darkness of the conifers.

Parc Mawr is a strip of ancient woodland occupying the steep slopes of the valley where agriculture has been of limited viability. Unfortunately, conifers were introduced in 1960 and are now threatening the native species which include ash, oak, cherry and elm. These trees still exist here but in dwindling numbers.

The tiny church of St Celynin

Another threat comes from invasive sycamore, a non-native species which tends to suppress the native trees and flowers of the area. Despite this, the woods still have a rich variety of wild flowers which include: bluebell, red campion, gold saxifrage, primrose, bugle, dog's mercury, celandine and wood anemone.

The Woodland Trust now owns and manages Parc Mawr and has introduced a programme to re-establish native broadleaf species. They also maintain a network of permissive footpaths which run throughout the wood.

3. At the bottom of the slope a large gate leads out of the woods and onto an access track. Turn right and follow the track past Nant-y-Coed to enter fields again by a stile just beyond the house. Keep to the left-hand field edge and bear left through the first gate in the wall. Turn right into a second field and then walk diagonally down the field to a ladder stile which leads onto a narrow access road.

Turn left, follow the access road to a T junction and turn right along a quiet lane. Walk along the lane and look for a signed field path on the left after about 200 yards. Keep to the field edge and climb a ladder stile in the field corner (ignore a stile to the left here). Turn right and walk along the field edge to a second stile which leads onto an access road. Bear right along the road and just before a gate turn left over stone steps and ladder stile into fields again. Turn right immediately and pass through a gap in the hedge, then walk through the centre of a field to a large metal gate beside farm buildings. Beyond the gate a road leads back to the Ty Gwyn Hotel.

6. Caerhun

Distance: *3½ miles*

Start: From Tal-y-Cafn take the B5279 to Ty'n-y-Groes. This crosses over the river before climbing to the village. About 250 yards or so after the road begins to climb there is a lay-by on the right where a few cars may be parked.
Grid ref. 783 718 (Ordnance Survey Outdoor Leisure Map 17).

The Route

1. Walk back to the main road and turn left down the hill. After about 200 yards, turn right onto a farm access road which runs parallel to the river. Continue to Tal-y-Cafn Uchaf (farm) following the track through the farmyard. Just before the final outbuildings, the track splits; keep right here and walk through a large hay shed to enter fields by a large gate. Keep to the left-hand field edge now and enter a small wood (Coed yr Arw) by a ladder stile.

The name of this wood recalls a group of rocks in the nearby river which were known as Yr Arw—'the roughness'. This reef proved to be quite a hazard and limited the size of craft that could safely navigate the river. It was removed by blasting at the beginning of the nineteenth century.

Follow a well worn footpath through the trees to enter fields again. Walk directly through the centre of a large field aiming for the left-hand end of a small wood. Keep right beside the fence and join a farm track after a second small wood. Bear right (straight ahead!) along the track and continue to Caerhun Church.

This is the site of Canovium, a Roman fort of the first and second centuries AD. It covers almost two hectares and occupied a site of great strategic importance, commanding what was then the lowest

52

crossing point on the river, one of the major obstacles on the road from *Deva* (Chester) to *Segontium* (Caernarfon). From here the road continued west over Bwlch-y-Ddeufaen above Rowen, down to Abergwyngregyn and then along the coastal plain to *Segontium*. The fort is thought to have originally been built as part of Agricola's Welsh campaign of AD 77 to house a garrison of about 500 men.

When the site was excavated in 1926-9 it was found to consist of a stone wall protecting the usual range of buildings: headquarters

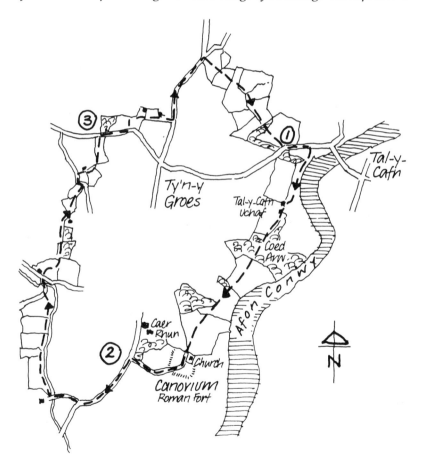

and commander's house (which now lie beneath the road where it leaves the enclosure near the south west corner); barrack blocks (covered by the church and cemetery) and granaries situated in the field to the right of the car park.

Our entry into the site marks the approximate location of the north gate. There was also a south gate on the opposite side of the enclosure, with evidence of a large civilian settlement on the flat land to the south. These 'shanty towns' were common at many Roman forts, particularly in Wales where large towns were almost nonexistent.

Beyond the church follow the tarmac lane to the main road (B5106).

2. Turn left and walk along the road until the gradient levels and there is a small lay-by on the left. Just beyond this, cross over and turn right down a concrete farm road. Immediately before the farm, the road crosses Afon Roe and a stile on the right leads into fields. Follow the right of way through several fields well supplied with stiles with the river on your right. In the final field, bear half-left away from the river and rise to a stile in the top corner of the field with a cottage on the right.

Turn right here and follow a quiet lane over the bridge at Pontwgan. Go through a metal gate directly opposite (footpath sign) and walk past a small stone cottage on the left, bearing right by the outbuildings. After a gate pass through a gap in the hedge and in the second field turn left and look for a ladder stile in the top corner. Walk directly through the following field to a metal stile at the left-hand corner of a small wood. Immediately after the stile, climb over iron railings and keep to the right along the field edge. Pass a house on the right, go through a large gate and walk directly through the following two fields to where a gate leads into a narrow lane.

Afon Conwy near Caerhun

Turn left down the lane and after 50 yards look for an access track on the right (footpath sign). Walk down the track passing a stone cottage on the right. The original right of way lies along a short enclosed track immediately opposite the cottage but this is no longer passable, so go through the gate immediately ahead, turn left and join the right of way about halfway down the field. After a few yards, you reach a junction of walls and a gate, directly ahead leads into a large field. Go through the gate and enter a lane by a gate in the top left-hand corner of the field.

3. Turn right along the lane and opposite the driveway to Bryn Derw, a wooden ladder stile on the left leads into fields again. Walk directly through the field to a stile but don't climb over, instead, turn right and walk along the field edge to where a gate leads onto a farm track. Turn sharp right here and instead of following the farm track, go through a second gate on the right which leads onto a footpath enclosed by high hedgerows. At the end of the path join the farm road and continue to the main road (B5106).

Turn left along the road and after about ¼ mile and just after the entrance to Wern Caravan Park, look for a ladder stile on the right. This is just before a left-hand bend and narrow lane on the right. Walk directly through the centre of the field to a stile beside a gate. Take a direct line through the following fields and after the next stile keep right along the field edge. Another stile now leads into two large grazing fields separated by a fence. Keep right again and look for a stile in the corner of the second field which leads into a narrow finger of woodland. Pass through the trees and cut directly through the centre of the following large field. A metal ladder stile leads into the lay-by to complete the route.

7. Dolgarrog

Distance: *5 miles*

Start: There is parking available on the B5106 in the village of Tal-y-Bont, 1¼ miles south of Ty'n-y-Groes. Park in a lay-by just before The Lodge Hotel.
Grid ref. 768 694 (Ordnance Survey Outdoor Leisure Map 17).

The Route

1. Walk south along the road passing The Lodge Hotel and turn right into a minor lane by a public house ('Y Bedol'). Pass playing fields on the left and just before the Llanbedr-y-cennin sign, turn left down an unmade access road. Where the road bends right towards a white house, go through a wooden kissing gate directly ahead and walk through a small boulder strewn grazing area to a ladder stile.

Follow the right of way along the wooded bank of a broad rocky stream (Afon Dulyn). Two more stiles take you into an overgrown green lane. Turn left here and cross the stream by a footbridge, then rise to a lane. Turn left down the lane for a few yards, then look for a signed footpath on the right which cuts through a small field to enter woods. The line of the right of way is not visible on the ground, but is indicated by yellow paint marks on trees. It takes a direct line contouring the slope.

Enter into a steeply sloping grazing field. If you have taken the correct route through the woods, there should be yellow paint marks on fence posts here but no stile. Contour the field to enter woods again. Take care to enter the trees at the correct point marked by two yellow posts (no stile again). As before, the line of the right of way is not visible on the ground, but yellow paint marks indicate the route. Contour the slope following the paint marks through the trees and climb over a second fence by a yellow arrow on a tree just after a stream. Make a slight rise from here, then continue through the trees following the markers until the path splits at a ruined stone wall (not very distinct). Take the right fork uphill between walls and at a T junction turn right. Walk up a green lane to a house on the left and bear right along the tarmac access road. Follow the road up the hill passing more houses.

2. At a T junction, turn left and follow a lane to the bridge over the outflow from the Coedty Reservoir (about ½ mile).

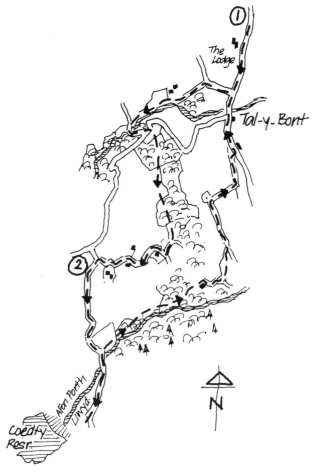

Coedty Reservoir

In November 1925 a torrent of water and boulders swept down this valley and plunged into the ravine below engulfing the village of Porth-lwyd and part of Dolgarrog. The water came from Llyn Eigiau, over four miles away where the dam had been breached by heavy rains. This overloaded the Coedty dam which also burst releasing a torrent which plunged 800 feet to the valley.

The flood engulfed part of the aluminium works at Dolgarrog causing some of the furnaces to explode, killing several workers. The church and the settlement of Porth-llwyd were completely destroyed, although at the time, most of the children were in the local cinema at Dolgarrog which was clear of the course of the water. In all, sixteen villagers lost their lives. Debris from the flood is still evident in the form of huge boulders which lie close to the road at the northern end of the village.

The aluminium works dates from 1907 and was sited here to make use of hydroelectric power, generated by means of reservoirs high in the hills above the village.

This road leads up to the Coedty Reservoir (½ mile), where a bridleway continues to Llyn Eigiau (about 4 miles each way) and the lonely cwm above (6 miles each way). If you visit any of the above lakes return to this point to continue the walk.

Scattered about these higher pastures are numerous ruined hill farms, many still carrying the name 'hafod'. Their counterpart in the valley is identified by the name 'hendre', a name which is also still common. They are a legacy from an agricultural system which saw the movement of an entire family and their animals from valley to mountain pasture during spring and summer, then back to the valley for the winter months. In many ways this method still continues but the two farms are now worked from the greater comfort of the valley. The name 'hafod' will be seen referring most often to abandoned ruins high in the hills.

Turn back down the lane and after a short rise turn right over a ladder stile. This path is well worn and easily followed to a point were the slope steepens and the stream falls between huge fallen boulders. After this, the path veers away from the stream to cross a ladder stile. Beyond the stile the path splits; keep right here following a path between ruined stone walls. Cross an access road beside a house on the right and take the footpath opposite which curves left through the trees.

At the bottom of the slope, a kissing gate leads into a lane. Turn left along the lane and continue through a farm and down to the road opposite the post office in Tal-y-Bont. Turn left along the road and return to point 1.

8. Maenan

Distance: *3 miles*

Start: There is a small National Trust car park in Maenan provided for the Cadair Ifan Goch viewpoint and walk. This can be reached by taking the minor lane signed "Cadair Ifan Goch" opposite The Priory Hotel and Maenan Abbey Caravan Site and keeping left at the first fork.
Grid ref. 795 665 (Ordnance Survey Outdoor Leisure Map 17).

The Route

1. Leave the car park by the kissing gate located behind the information board. Follow the obvious forestry road until, after rising and curving leftwards, you reach a junction of paths. Turn right here signed "Cadair Ifan Goch". Follow the path for about 300 yards to the National Trust sign. Here you can make a short detour to the left to the Cadair Ifan Goch viewpoint.

Cadair Ifan Goch—'Red John's Chair', takes its name from a legendary red haired giant who is said to sit here to bathe his feet in the soothing waters of Afon Conwy. Today, visitors are attracted by one of the finest viewpoints in the area. At almost 500 feet above the valley floor, you are treated to a wide panorama in both directions—from Ty'n-y-Groes in the north, to the wooded profile of Parc Uchaf above Llanrwst. Opposite, the steep valley sides above Dolgarrog rise to the remote hanging valleys of the eastern Carneddau.

It was to this central section of the valley that the monks of Aberconwy Abbey were relocated when Edward I chose the site of their abbey for his new castle and town. Aberconwy had been granted to the Cistercians by Llywelyn Fawr, said to have been a religious man who regularly attended the church at Llanrhychwyn (route 9) above Trefriw with his wife Princess Joan. A new abbey

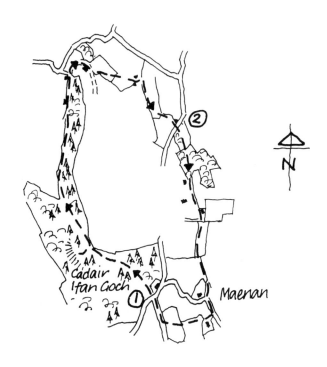

was built for the monks at Maenan and most of their privileges were transferred. They remained here until Henry VIII dissolved the monasteries in 1536.

Many buildings escaped complete destruction during the Dissolution but not Maenan, nothing of the original building remains today. Most of the stone was taken away by Henry's officials to repair Caernarfon Castle, although some materials are thought have been used in the construction of nearby Gwydir by the Wynn family. The Wynn chapel at Llanrwst church contains a carved rood-screen thought to have come from the abbey, as well as part of a stone coffin said to be that of Llywelyn Fawr (Llywelyn ap Iorwerth). It seems the monks took the remains of their patron with them when they moved to Maenan.

Return to the path by the National Trust sign and turn left. This path soon becomes a well defined track which descends gradually to a kissing gate. Go through the gate and follow the track past houses on your left. Lower down, the track becomes an unsurfaced road which bends sharp left beyond the final house. On the curve of the bend, turn right through a large metal gate and walk along a grassy farm track to a second gate. Pass farm buildings on the right and immediately after a kissing gate, bear left off the track onto a faint footpath which runs beside a stream on the left. This path takes you to a footbridge over the stream and a kissing gate. Beyond the gate, turn right up the bank and cut

Cadair Ifan Goch

through the centre of a field to another kissing gate. Take a direct line through the following field towards a small farm. Walk through the farmyard passing the house on your left and continue up the drive. After about 40 yards, turn right onto a second farm track and follow this to a fork at the top of the rise. Keep left through the gate here and in the second field turn right towards a small cottage. Go through a kissing gate to the right of the cottage and walk down the drive to the lane.

2. Directly opposite, a finger post indicates the continuation of the footpath. Keep to the right-hand edge of the field and in the top right corner, a kissing gate leads into woods. Follow the path directly ahead through the trees and join a rough farm track near a ruin on the right. Follow the track past a farm on the right and continue to a second farm. Pass the front of the farmhouse and continue straight ahead to a metal gate with outbuildings to the right. Go through the gate and keep to the right-hand field edge. In the corner of the field, a gate takes you into a second field. Keep to the left-hand field edge and look for a small metal gate which leads into a small wood with a garden on your right. Walk through the wood to a lane and turn right down the hill.

At a T junction turn left and walk along the lane to a signed public footpath which uses the driveway to Tan-y-Graig. Walk down the drive and continue straight ahead where this curves left after a few yards. Enter fields and keep straight ahead to a kissing gate in the right-hand corner of the field. Walk directly ahead to another kissing gate which leads into the lane. Turn right here and return to the car park.

9. Trefriw and Llanrwst

Distance: *5½ miles*

Start: There is a large free car park in Llanrwst just over the old bridge (Pont Fawr) on the B5106.
Grid ref. 798 614 (Ordnance Survey Outdoor Leisure Map 17).

The Route

1. Turn right out of the car park and walk along the road towards the old bridge. Immediately before the tearooms and gift shop, cross the road and take the signed footpath on the left.

One of the most distinctive features of Llanrwst is its bridge; 'Pont Fawr' (the 'Large Bridge'), which has spanned the river since 1636. Its height can be explained by the need to avoid frequent floods which sweep down from the mountains. Originally the central span was even higher but this collapsed and had to be rebuilt in the 1670s.

The town developed around the bridge which, until the early nineteenth century, provided the lowest river crossing in the valley. This meant that travellers en-route from London to Holyhead had to pass through Llanrwst and numerous hotels and inns were built during the late eighteenth century to cater for them. Much of this trade was lost to Betws-y-Coed when Thomas Telford built what is now the A5, along with a new bridge just above the town.

The parish church, which can be seen across the river, is famous for containing the carved stone coffin of Llywelyn ap Iorwerth (Llywelyn Fawr). Llywelyn had close associations with the Conwy Valley and founded the abbey at Aberconwy where he died in 1240. When Edward I moved the monks to Maenan to make way for his new castle, they took with them the coffin of their patron, but it disappeared when the abbey was pulled down during the

Dissolution. The lower half has since been recovered and now resides in the Wynn chapel. The coffin of his wife, Princess Joan has also survived and can be seen in the doorway of Beaumaris church on Anglesey.

Follow the path for some distance between fields. Where the path bends sharply to the left, ignore a ladder stile on the right, instead, continue to the next bend and cross the stile directly ahead to enter a large field. Keep right beside the fence and at the road turn right.

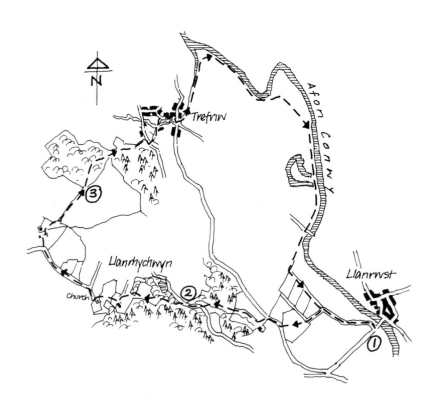

Nearby is the Tudor mansion of Gwydir, seat of the Wynn family since 1500. The Wynns came to Gwydir from Dolwyddelan in the Lledr valley after purchasing the estate from a descendant of Llywelyn Fawr (Llywelyn ap Iorwerth).

The present house was built by John Wynn in 1555 and is a fine example of Tudor building, although some of its stone work, particularly window and door surrounds, appear to have been dressed for another purpose; possibly coming from the demolition of nearby Maenan Abbey.

The most famous (or infamous) member of the Wynn family is the first baronet, Sir John Wynn (1554-1627). His pursuit of wealth and prominence resulted in numerous local enterprises, such as lead mining in the hills around Llyn Geirionydd and the improvement of Afon Conwy to make it navigable to small commercial craft. He also ruthlessly exploited his tenants to the extent that several of his neighbours brought legal cases against him. He is reputed to have used his political influence to obtain a pardon.

Walk along the road for about 200 yards and look for a signed footpath on the left beside the driveway to 'Glan Gors'. Follow the path which is enclosed at first, then, after a ladder stile bear half-right up a bracken covered bank. Turn left over a second stile at the top of the bank and keep right walking parallel to the wall. In the top corner of the field, an iron kissing gate leads through an area of bracken to a large metal gate at the edge of woods. Go through the gate and turn left along a track for a few yards before bearing right onto a narrow footpath which cuts directly up through the trees. This footpath is marked by yellow paint spots on trees.

Higher up the hillside, the path makes a short descent to the left (follow the paint marks) to cross a stream by means of stones and two fallen trees (some walkers may find this crossing difficult, if so continue directly uphill through the trees to the lane). Beyond the stream, follow the yellow markers up the bank to the lane.

Pont Fawr, Llanrwst

2. Turn right and walk up the lane for about 200 yards and just before the tiny bridge over the stream, take the signed footpath on the left. After a ladder stile follow the faint remains of a farm track along the edge of a small field, then through an open oak wood. A gate leads into a small field and the track continues straight ahead towards a farm. Just before the farm, join the access road and turn left towards the house. Immediately adjacent to the farmhouse, turn right up steps signed to 'Llanrhychwyn Church'. At the top of the field go through a kissing gate and bear left up the field to a second kissing gate in the wall. Turn left to visit Llanrhychwyn church.

This ancient church, reminiscent of the tiny church of St Celynin above Rowen (route 6), is said to be one of the oldest churches in Britain with parts of the building (about half its present form) dating back to the eleventh century, the time of Llywelyn ap Iorwerth (Llywelyn the Great). Traditionally, it is said to have been used by Llywelyn and his wife Princess Joan, daughter of King John, but in her later years Joan found the long walk so tiring that Llywelyn had St Mary's church in Trefriw built for her convenience in 1230. The present form of the church dates from the eighteenth century, when a number of alterations were carried out.

From the church gate turn left to a kissing gate in the field corner and turn right along the farm access road. At the T junction turn left, signposted 'Llyn Geirionydd'. Follow the lane for several hundred yards and, immediately after a gate across the road, turn right down a driveway lined with pine trees. Just before the house turn right, then bear left and at a T junction turn right again. Keep right at a second T junction and immediately after the next gate, turn left up the bank. There are numerous sheep tracks here but the right of way keeps parallel to the fence on the left. Continue to a broad col at the top of the rise.

From this point, a short detour can be made by rising to the top of the rocky knoll on the left for a fine view of the surrounding countryside. Walkers are reminded that there is **no right of way** here, but the footpath appears to be well used and there seems to be no objection to its use.

The view takes in the Geirionydd and Crafnant valleys, with Moel Siabod peeping over the wooded slopes of Mynydd Deulyn. To the north, the hills plunge steeply into the Conwy Valley with the village of Trefriw at your feet.

3. Return to the col and look for a ladder stile over the wall on the left. This leads onto a good path which drops steeply through the bracken. As the woods thicken, the path becomes less indistinct and curves right to join a well worn path at a T junction. Turn right and follow the path to a stile in the lower right-hand corner of the wood. This leads into a small conifer plantation and a good path takes you down to the

69

road. Turn right along the road and after about 75 yards, look for a footpath sign on the left. Follow this path and where it joins the lane, keep left down the hill. Go straight across at the next junction and cross the river by the footbridge. Keep right after the bridge and at the road turn right. At the first junction keep right again and walk down the hill to the main road opposite the Fairy Falls Hotel.

The name Trefriw is thought to mean 'healing town'— undoubtedly a reference to the town's mineral rich waters which have been exploited since Roman times.

Before the Industrial Revolution, Trefriw was a prominent trading centre and had the distinction of being the largest inland port in the whole of Wales. Goods were brought up the river by boat to a nearby quay and returned with slate, ore and timber from the hills above the town. It was also a centre for the local wool trade with the nearby mill established to wash and finish cloth already woven by cottagers. This was known as a 'fulling' mill or Pandy.

During the nineteenth century, Victorian visitors came in their thousands to take the sulphur and iron rich waters which enabled the town to develop as a spa and curative centre. These visitors were often brought by steamer from Conwy, Llandudno and Deganwy—up to 1,000 visitors per day were recorded. The steamer service continued until the Second World War when it was abandoned due to silting of the river.

Turn right and cross the road by Trefriw Woollen Mill. Take the signed footpath on the left now by the public toilets. This follows the river for about two miles.

After the suspension bridge, continue beside the river for about 400 yards to a stile. Cross the stile and bear left to a second stile. A well used footpath takes a direct line through the following fields well supplied with stiles. This path eventually joins the footpath used earlier in the walk. Turn left and retrace your route back to the car park at point 1.

10. Llyn Crafnant

Distance: *5 miles*

Start: Llyn Crafnant can be reached by following the signed lane from Trefriw opposite the Fairy Falls Hotel. Parking is available in a large Forest Enterprises car park. WC facilities are provided and a parking fee is required.
Grid ref. 757 618 (Ordnance Survey Outdoor Leisure Map 17).

The Route

1. Turn right out of the car park and walk up the road to the lake.

This will be your first view of Llyn Crafnant and the beautiful valley that encloses it. The name Crafnant is possibly derived from the words 'craf'—which refers to garlic and 'nant'—a valley or gorge. If this is the case, the name Crafnant means: 'gorge or valley of garlic'.

A column near the outflow of the lake records the gift made by Richard James of Dyffryn Aur to Llanrwst Parish Council in 1895, enabling them to take a water supply from the lake.

Turn right just before the lake, pass through a kissing gate and bear left onto a forestry track which keeps close to the water's edge for some distance. Keep left at a fork in the track about half way along the lake.

At the head of the lake the track becomes rougher and rises towards 'Hendre', an old farmhouse below the path on the left. Just before the house, bear left down the bank to a stile and walk past the house and a smaller converted barn (Hendre Bach) to join the access track over a footbridge on the right (ignore a stile on the left here). Turn left along the track passing two white-washed wooden houses and at the end of the track turn left through a large metal gate onto the tarmac lane. Follow the lane for about ½ mile.

2. Immediately before a telephone box, bear right onto a signed footpath ("Llyn Geirionydd"). After about 200 yards you meet the path from 'Cynllwyd', turn right here and follow the well worn path over the shoulder of Mynydd Deulyn.

At the top of the rise, a stile leads over the wall and a short drop brings you to a forestry road. Walk down the hill for a few yards and where the road forks, look for a footpath directly ahead (between the two forest roads). This path heads

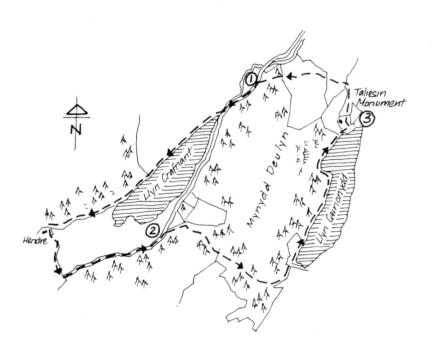

directly downhill crossing the forest road twice before you arrive at a T junction with fields ahead. Turn left along the track and where this bends right, look for a stile on the left. After the stile, walk through a field with the waters of Llyn Geirionydd to the right. Enter the woods again and continue along the water's edge for about ¾ mile.

Sadly, this beautiful lake has become a casualty of the local mining industry. Its waters have been poisoned by lead and other minerals seeping from nearby waste and are almost sterile.

As you approach the end of the lake, leave the woods behind and follow the footpath to a small stone barn on the right. Turn left along the access road to a house and after 20 yards or so turn right (waymarker). Walk up to a stone monument and look back for a fine view of Llyn Geirionydd and the steep hillside of Mynydd Deulyn.

The monument was erected in 1850 by Lord Willoughby d' Eresby of nearby Gwydir to commemorate the supposed birthplace of Taliesin, the famous sixth century bard. Numerous stories surround this mystical character but perhaps the best known is his association with King Maelgwyn Gwynedd. Maelgwyn, who ruled from 510-547, was the great-grandson of Cunedda, the powerful chieftain who came down from one of the northern British kingdoms in the fifth century to rid Wales of Irish invaders and establish the kingdom of Gwynedd. By the time of Maelgwyn the Irish threat had gone and he was able to use a period of relative peace to indulge in a life of extravagance and luxury rare among his contemporaries.

He built a palace at Deganwy on a hilltop known today as The Vardre, which overlooks the mouth of Afon Conwy but his lifestyle soon brought condemnation and he was declared to be one of the most 'sinful rulers' of his day by the monk Gildas, a sixth century chronicler and contemporary.

Despite his failings, Maelgwyn was a lover of music and poetry and harboured many musicians and bards at his court. On one

73

Llyn Crafnant

occasion, his nephew Elffin came to visit and brought with him his bard, the great Taliesin. Maelgwyn's famous temper flared during the visit and the two parted as enemies. Taliesin's parting gift to Maelgwyn was to foretell his death—"a creature would rise from Morfa Rhianedd (the plain on which Llandudno is now built) to punish him, 'its hair, its teeth and its eyes are yellow and this makes an end of Maelgwyn Gwynedd.'"

74

Maelgwyn is said to have been so terrified that he locked himself into the church at Llanrhos but unable to resist his curiosity, he looked through the keyhole, saw the creature waiting and died on the spot.

This story though fanciful, may have some elements of fact. Maelgwyn is known to have died in 547, possibly of the yellow plague which swept Europe during the mid sixth century. With news of its progress through Britain, Maelgwyn may have anticipated his fate and retired to the nearby church to die.

The Taliesin Monument is also noted for its associations with the Eisteddfod organised by the bard Gwilym Cowlyd (real name William John Roberts), in the second half of the nineteenth century. He worked as a poet, printer and bookseller and published the works of a number of fellow poets. As a bard he was highly respected and won the Chair at the National Eisteddfod at Conwy in 1861. His high standards led him into disagreement with the rules, so together with an associate, he organised a rival Eisteddfod in 1863 under the name of 'Arwest Glan Geirionydd'. The location was here around the Taliesin monument for obvious reasons and for a while it rivalled the National Eisteddfod in popularity, attracting entries from all over Wales.

When Gwilym died in 1904 at the age of 76, the great driving force behind the event was gone. It was held for the last time in 1912.

3. Follow the path beyond the monument and keep to the right of a small group of conifers. Beyond the trees the path drops to cross a stone wall on the left by a stile. After the stile, keep left at a fork and follow a rising path which eventually passes through an area of old mines. A stile now leads onto a forestry road which soon forks; keep right here down the hill and at the road return to the car park.

11. Betws-y-Coed—Llyn Parc

Distance: *4½ miles*

Start: There are a number of car parks along with street parking available in Betws-y-Coed. Begin the walk at the old stone bridge carrying the B5106 over Afon Llugwy (opposite Climber & Rambler outdoor shop).
Grid ref. 792 568 (Ordnance Survey Outdoor Leisure Map 17).

The Route

1. Cross the river and take the first road on the left immediately after the bridge. After about 30 yards there is a pay and display car park on your right; bear left here and follow the riverside footpath for about ¾ mile.

As the river narrows and its banks become more wooded, a small gorge is entered and a wooden footbridge known as the 'Miner's Bridge' spans the river.

The 'Miner's Bridge', along with the nearby 'Miner's Arms' recalls the occupation of many locals when lead mining was carried out in the numerous mines of the Gwydir Forest during the nineteenth century. The original bridge provided a short-cut for miners living at Pentre Du on the south side of the river saving them the mile and a half walk via the old bridge at Betws-y-Coed.

Do not cross the Miner's Bridge, instead bear right up the hillside and rise to a lane. A footpath sign indicates the continuation of the footpath opposite. This well used and obvious footpath runs diagonally-left up the hillside for some distance. At the top of the rise the path zig-zags up to a stile which leads into fields. Take the path directly ahead marked by blue tipped posts and cross the access road to a farm on the left. Opposite, the path continues up the bank past a ruin on the left to a second stile after about 75 yards.

There are good views to the west from here. The most dominant peak is Moel Siabod with the summits of the Snowdon group to the right at the head of Dyffryn Mymbyr. The serrated summit ridge of Tryfan can be seen peeping over the shoulder of the Glyders to the right.

2. Cross the stile and walk beside a conifer plantation on the right to a ladder stile which leads onto a forestry road. Turn left (ignore a track immediately on the left which leads back into fields) and follow the road which curves right through an area of young conifers. Ignore a track on the left immediately before spoil heaps and mine workings, instead continue to a sharp left-hand bend with grazing fields directly ahead. Immediately after the bend, bear half-right up the

The Miner's Bridge

bank following a footpath marked by blue tipped posts. At the top of the bank climb a ladder stile, turn right and follow an enclosed footpath. Two stiles take you across a gate between fields and the enclosed footpath continues with woods to the right. A stile at the end of the path leads into a field and a track heads towards a stone house ('Coedmawr').

78

Turn left onto a track which passes in front of the house and continue through a small field to a ladder stile beside outbuildings in the far corner. Turn right immediately after the stile and at a junction of forest roads turn right again. Follow this road for some distance ignoring a prominent track on the left. About 200 yards beyond this, look for a path on the left which leaves the road opposite two blue tipped posts on the right. This path rises slightly before dropping to another forest road. Turn left and walk down the road to the outflow of Llyn Parc.

Mining in this area has a history which reaches back almost four centuries and began with Sir John Wynn, from nearby Gwydir, who encouraged entrepreneurs to test the viability of mineral lodes on his estate in the early 1600s. Ore was exported from a quay in nearby Trefriw on a small scale at first but expanded to become a major industry in the area by the early nineteenth century. By the turn of the twentieth century however, the mines were in decline, although high world market prices for zinc blende prompted the reopening of several mines until the 1920s.

By World War II only Parc Mine (at the northern end of the lake) was still in operation. It was modernised and a new processing plant, enabling ores with a low metallic content to be worked, was installed. This operated until the 1960s when it finally ceased operations.

The principal ores found here are lead (Galena) and zinc (Blende). These are found in steeply inclined fissures or 'lodes', formed during a period of intense volcanic activity when intrusions were made into mudstones laid down during the Ordovician period.

Today the Gwydir mines form part of the Gwydir Forest owned by the Forestry Commission, who have developed the Miner's Trail in the area of greatest activity to the north of Llyn Parc. The trail is waymarked with a symbol and is supplied with interpretation boards explaining the area's history.

3. From Llyn Parc, retrace your steps back up the forest road for about 100 yards to where blue tipped posts again mark a footpath on the left. This is just after a small field on the left opposite the lake. The path is quite narrow but well walked and its line is clearly marked by the posts. After a descent, a short rise is made via wooden steps and the path takes you right along the top of the hill overlooking a gorge on your left to join a well made forest road.

Follow this road with fine views down into the Conwy Valley until it begins to curve right towards an area of fields and farm buildings with a grand view of Moel Siabod directly ahead. Immediately on the left here, a blue post and handrail indicate a narrow but well used footpath which drops into the trees. Follow this and at the next junction turn left onto a good forest road.

Follow this road until it ends in a circular turning area. A few yards before this, bear right onto a footpath marked again by blue tipped posts. This is well used and eventually drops to a T junction. Take the signed path on the left which drops for some distance and eventually zig-zags close to the rocks of Clogwyn Cyrrau. At the bottom of the hill turn left onto a forest road and after about 60 yards turn right onto a footpath beside a black wooden shed. This drops to a lane where a right turn takes you shortly to a T junction. Turn left here and walk back into Betws-y-Coed.

12. Betws-y-Coed—Llyn Elsi

Distance: *3¾ miles*

Start: As for route 11.
Grid ref. 792 568 (Ordnance Survey Outdoor Leisure Map 17).

The Route

1. Cross the river and take the first road on the left immediately after the bridge. After about 30 yards there is a pay and display car park on your right; bear left here and follow the riverside footpath for about ¾ mile.

Afon Llugwy drains the eastern mountains of northern Snowdonia, including much of the Ogwen valley and Dyffryn Mymbyr. In its journey east to join the Conwy it has carved the only breach in a high plateau area and has thus been used as a major communication route for centuries. Betws-y-Coed owes its existence to the use of this route as part of the London to Holyhead road during the eighteenth century.

As the river narrows and its banks become more wooded, a gorge is entered and a wooden footbridge, known as the "Miner's Bridge", takes you over to the far bank.

The name of this bridge recalls the occupation of many of the locals when lead mining was carried out on the plateau to the north during the nineteenth century. The original bridge provided a short-cut for miners living at Pentre Du on the south side of the river, thus saving them the mile and a half walk via the old bridge at Betws-y-Coed.

2. Beyond the bridge, steps take you out of the rocky bed of the river and a short walk brings you to the A5. Cross the road and take the access road opposite turning right almost immediately. A short rise brings you to the car park for the "Garth Falls Walk". Turn left off the road here and follow the signed path to "Rhiwddolion", a deserted mining village high on the hills above Betws-y-Coed.

The path follows a stream on your left before bearing right just before a small waterfall. At a T junction with a prominent forestry road, turn left and follow the road over the stream passing a house on the right. About 120 yards beyond the house, look for a narrow but well used footpath on the right. This weaves through an area of felled trees and thicker woods to emerge in a small field (stile) with spoil heaps from disused mine workings on your right. Walk through the field keeping right and cross the stile in the lower right-hand corner. Turn right, then immediately left passing the ruins of mine buildings on the right, to cross a stream which issues from an old adit.

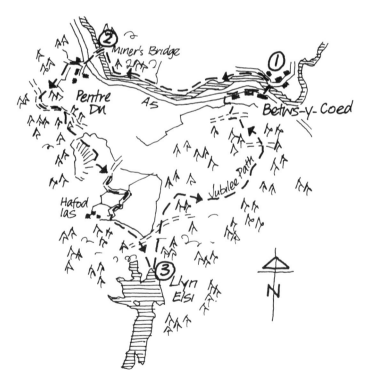

Looking across the Llugwy valley from below Hafod-las

These spoil heaps and deserted buildings are the remains of Hafod-las slate quarry, which operated during the last century. It was worked by the men of Pentre Du and the now deserted village of Rhiwddolion, situated on the plateau above the quarry.

At the top of the rise bear left and after about 75 yards, turn right at a T junction. Follow the prominent path which bends sharp left by a deep quarry on the right and, beyond a gate, continues to rise to an old barn with fields to the left. Climb over the stile here, turn right and continue the climb towards Hafod-las (farm) with views of the valley and the eastern Carneddau to the right.

At the top of the rise and just before the farm, turn sharp left as indicated by a waymark and skirt the conifer plantations to your right. A little further on, a stile on the right takes you into the trees. Follow the obvious footpath for some distance and at a forestry road cross over. This path makes its way to the memorial stone overlooking Llyn Elsi.

This elevated lake surrounded by woods, makes a fine foreground for panoramic views of Snowdonia's highest summits but not Snowdon itself which is hidden behind Moel Siabod, the most prominent peak in the view. To the right are the Glyders, with Tryfan's serrated outline peeping over the shoulder of Galt yr Ogof. Across the Ogwen valley, rise the rounded and often snow covered slopes of the Carneddau.

The memorial stone was erected to commemorate the opening of a new water supply from Llyn Elsi, by Betws-y-Coed UDC on June 18 1914.

3. Stand with the memorial to your back and, facing the path which you have just used, take the next well worn footpath in a clockwise direction (at about 2 o'clock and almost due north). At the time of writing, this path is marked by wooden posts and crosses the open moors for a short distance before entering the trees again. Cross a forestry road taking the footpath opposite and continue on this path for some distance, crossing a second forest road about half way down the hillside.

After a short rise, the path levels and joins a grassy track. After 100 yards or so bear right into the trees at a fork. Almost at the A5 and within earshot of the traffic, turn left at a T junction and after about 30 yards turn right onto a narrow footpath which soon brings you to the road. Turn right now and walk back through Betws-y-Coed to your starting point.

Betws-y-Coed owes its existence to the use of the Llugwy and Ogwen valleys by the London to Holyhead road and the growing popularity of travelling for its own sake—a trend begun in the eighteenth century by individuals like Thomas Pennant. Prior to this it was a small hamlet gathered around the old bridge—Pont-y-Pair, thought to have been built in the fifteenth century. The church of St Michael, situated near the junction of the Llugwy and Conwy, is of great antiquity and dates from the fourteenth century.

The name Betws-y-Coed means the 'oratory in the wood', possibly a reference to a chapel on the old 'Saints Road' to Bardsey during the Middle Ages. The old road must have passed this way because of the existence of nearby Ysbyty Ifan ('John's Hospital'), established by the 'Knights of the Order of St John of Jerusalem' as a hospice and resting place towards the end of the twelfth century.

Things changed rapidly in this isolated spot during the early nineteenth century when Thomas Telford came here to survey and improve the London to Holyhead road. A new bridge—Y Bont Haearn ('the Iron Bridge'), was built in 1815 to carry his new road over Afon Conwy. This passed through Betws-y-Coed bringing numerous visitors and most importantly, the Irish mail coach.

The coming of the railway in the mid-nineteenth century brought mixed blessings, it did away with the Irish mail coach (mail now went via the new rail line along the coast) but a new branch line, which came down the Conwy Valley from Llandudno Junction, brought many more tourists. Inns and hotels were built to accommodate and cater for travellers and visitors. By the turn of the century there were no fewer than 40 boarding houses and six hotels here.

Betws-y-Coed has remained popular, particularly with weekend and day visitors and its shops and hotels still cater for this market, although there has been little real development here since the end of the nineteenth century.

13. Moel Trefriw

Distance: *2¾ miles*

Start: Begin the walk in the little village of Capel Garmon situated high above the Conwy valley. There are no official car parks so take care with your parking. Start from the White Horse public house where cars can sometimes be left with the landlord's permission.
Grid ref. 816 554 (Ordnance Survey Outdoor Leisure Map 17).

The Route

1. With the post office on your left and the White Horse to your right, turn right immediately after the pub and pass the public toilets on your left. A few yards beyond this, turn left onto a paved path which passes in front of four small bungalows. Go through a kissing gate at the end of the path which leads into a small field. Keep to the right-hand field edge and walk towards a white stone farmhouse. Immediately in front of the house turn right onto an enclosed path which rises up the hillside. At the top of the rise, cross the stile and bear half-left to a second stile. Walk along the bank now with a few pine trees to your right before rising diagonally through the trees to cross a small field. After a kissing gate keep to the left-hand field edge to join a track which comes down from the right. Turn left then right over a ladder stile beside the ruins of Pen-y-ffridd (meaning 'head of the mountain pasture').

Walk directly up the field now keeping to the right-hand field edge. At the top of the rise there is a high point to your left.

At over 1,000 feet this hilltop gives dramatic views across the woods of the Conwy Valley to the mountains of Snowdonia. Unfortunately, Snowdon itself is not visible but is hidden behind

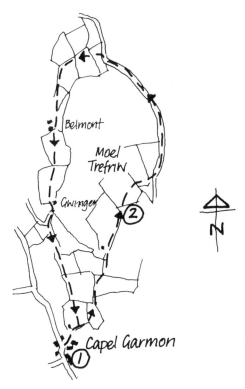

Moel Siabod which, being nearer than the other peaks appears to be one of the highest. To the right are the summits of the Glyder range with Tryfan's triple peak clearly visible. Further north are the rounded tops of the Carneddau, frequently snow covered in the winter months.

2. From here return to the path along the field edge, cross the bank (which you have been following as the field edge) and bear diagonally-left to a large metal gate. Walk diagonally-right across the following field (with an area of rough grass and marsh to your right) to a ladder stile which leads over the fence. Cut directly across the next small field aiming for two hawthorn bushes in the far fence. Beyond the bushes, a stile leads onto a farm track. Turn left and walk down the track with a deep valley to your right.

The minor road which follows the crest of the rounded ridge across the valley, was originally used as a coach road prior to Thomas Telford's improvement of what is now the A5. It passed through the village of Rhydlydan (now bypassed by the A5) and Pentrefoelas, then climbed to Nebo before making the long descent to Llanrwst where a crossing of one of North Wales' major barriers could be made—Afon Conwy. This formed part of the London to Holyhead road for a while and was built in the 1770s at the instigation, it is said, of an inn keeper from Shrewsbury by the name of Robert Lawrence. When the road was complete he immediately began a London to Holyhead coach service. With the improvement of the A5 and the building of a new bridge at Betws-y-Coed in 1815, this high route became obsolete. Today it is little used despite offering some of the best views in the whole of Wales.

Continue down the track (ignoring a path on the right) until it rounds the hillside to give a wide view north into the Conwy Valley. Lower down, the track steepens and after a couple of bends there is a kissing gate on the left which leads into fields again. Go through the gate and walk directly through the first field to a large metal gate, then take a similar line through the following field aiming for the far right-hand corner. Keep to field edges now heading for 'Belmont', a large house directly ahead. As you approach the house, go through a large gate into the yard and walk past the house and across a small car park to a kissing gate beside outbuildings on the right. This takes you into fields once again.

The rounded hillside to the right is the supposed site of a battle fought between Owain Maredydd of Deheubarth and the sons of Idwal Foel. Idwal Foel was Prince of Gwynedd and had been killed in battle with the English in 942. By Welsh law his sons should have succeeded him, instead the throne was seized by Hywel Dda the powerful ruler of Deheubarth in the south. After his death in 950, Idwal's sons set out to claim their rights and won a decisive battle against the south in 951. Three years later Maredydd attacked the north and fought a battle here above the Conwy Valley. He was defeated, but three of Idwal's sons also died in the battle.

Walk through the centre of the next two fields aiming for a stone farmhouse ('Gwinger') in the second field. Three gates to the right of the house take you through the yard to join an access road. Turn right along the road and at a sharp right-hand bend, bear left through a large metal gate. Take a direct line through several fields well supplied with gates and stiles, until you reach the cottage passed at the beginning of the walk. Retrace you steps back to Capel Garmon now.

Looking towards the mountains of Snowdonia, above Capel Garmon

14. Capel Garmon

Distance: *4½ miles*

Start: As for route 13.

Grid ref. 816 554 (Ordnance Survey Outdoor Leisure Map 17).

The route

1. With the White Horse on your left walk south along the lane out of the village. After about 600 yards the lane bends, there are metal railings on your right and the track to 'Bryn Ifan' on your left. A little further on, turn right over a ladder stile and walk along the left-hand field edge. A kissing gate leads into a second field and the right of way continues straight ahead towards a small farm ('Ty'n-y-coed'). Go through a large metal gate which leads into the yard and walk up the access road with the house on your right. After about 30 yards bear right onto a signed field path ('Capel Garmon Burial Chamber'). Keep right beside the hedge and about halfway along the field turn right through a gate. Bear diagonally-left across the field to the site of the burial chamber.

This is one of the best examples of a Neolithic Burial Chamber in the locality and also has one of the finest settings—backed by a panorama of Snowdonia's highest peaks. As with almost all such remains, the original mound which covered the site has been eroded but a line of stones enclosing the chamber mark its extremities. The remains consist of a triple chamber faced with dry-stone walling as well as large upright stones using a 'post and panel' technique. This has been extensively restored but original work can be seen in the lower courses of the eastern chamber. These were originally topped by large capstones but only one remains. In 1924 restoration work was carried out and steps taken to halt any further deterioration (in the previous century it had been used as a stable!).

90

Leave the site by the gate and turn right to a stile in the wall. Walk directly through the following two fields guided by footpath signs and a kissing gate, until you meet a farm track. Turn right along the track as directed by a footpath sign and follow it down the hill to Penrhyddion Ucha, a small hill farm with a view of Cwm Penmachno directly ahead. Walk through the farmyard and turn left at a T junction. After a few yards, turn sharp right and pass old stone outbuildings on your right. Go through the gate here and bear left across the stream to a second gate which leads into fields. Bear right down the field keeping to the right-hand edge and pass

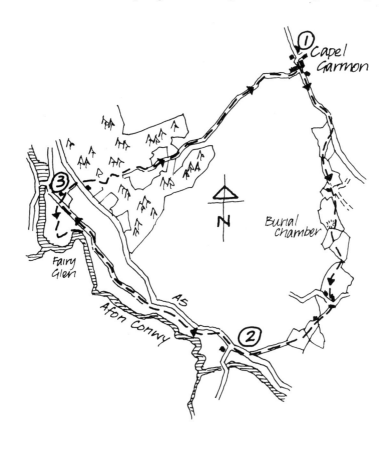

through a kissing gate on the right. Cross the stream and bear left through a small grazing field to a kissing gate in the wall which takes you into a camp site ('Rynys Camp Site'). Walk past the house, bear right onto the access road and follow this down the hill to the busy A5.

2. Turn right and walk along the road to the Conwy Falls Cafe and Restaurant. Take care on this section as there is no footpath and the road is often very busy. About 200 yards beyond the Cafe (just after the bend), bear left through a gap in the wall which takes you onto a well defined path with Afon Conwy down to your left.

This pleasant path is all that remains of the toll road built by the Capel Curig Turnpike Trust in the opening years of the nineteenth century. It provided a link between an earlier toll road (see previous route) which came to Pentrefoelas but then headed north to Llanrwst via Nebo and the road constructed by Lord Penrhyn between Bangor and Ty Hyll (the 'Ugly House', on what is now the A5 west of Betws-y-Coed). It crossed Afon Conwy at Pont yr Afanc, now used by the A470 Lledr Valley road and continued through Betws-y-Coed, thus providing a London to Holyhead road which avoided all the problems encountered on the coastal route via Conwy.

Stone embankments and buttresses can still be seen at various points along its length but it was still very narrow (rarely more than eight feet wide) and steep gradients made it both difficult and dangerous for coaches. It became redundant in 1815 when Thomas Telford built what is now the A5. Telford took a line higher up the hillside which was less steep (never more than 1:22) but he records in his diary that the section above the Conwy Falls (directly above) was the most difficult of the entire route through the mountains. Many early travellers, such as Thomas Pennant, would have passed along this 'old road' which seems to have remained in use for some time after the building of Telford's new road, as George Borrow records passing this way in 1862.

Lower down, the path widens into a broader track lined with oak and beech trees which would have clothed much of the valley during the Middle Ages. Continue until you come to the access path to Fairy Glen on the left. A small fee is payable by those who wish to visit Fairy Glen. Return to this point to continue the walk.

Fairy Glen became popular and acquired its English name during the Victorian period, when new roads allowed the nearby town of Betws-y-Coed to develop from a small hamlet on the Irish mail route, into a tourist destination in its own right. The Victorians revelled in the romantic landscape of the area and the walk to Fairy Glen became one of their most popular excursions.

3. Opposite the path to Fairy Glen, a ladder stile leads into a small field on the right with a stone cottage to the left. Keep to the field edge, cross a stile behind the cottage and bear right up the field to the A5. Cross the road and take the path between stone posts directly opposite (no stile). Climb steeply beside a stone wall at first, then zig-zag up through the trees until a forest road is reached and the angle eases considerably. Turn right along the forest road and follow this back to Capel Garmon.

15. Machno Falls

Distance: *5 miles*

Start: Begin the walk at the Conwy Falls Cafe and Restaurant. This is situated on the A5 at its junction with the B4406 Penmachno Road. A small parking fee is sometimes requested from those not using the cafe. Walkers using the cafe, either at the beginning or the end of their walk are welcome to park free of charge.
Grid ref. 811 535 (Ordnance Survey Outdoor Leisure Map 17).

The Route

1. Turn right out of the car park and walk along the Penmachno road (B4406) passing over Afon Conwy by Bont Newydd ('New Bridge'). This is the point at which the river enters a mile long gorge which contains both the Conwy Falls and Fairy Glen.

Continue along the lane to the Woollen Mill situated near a crossroads. Turn right and walk past the mill and over the old stone bridge spanning Afon Machno.

To the right you will see an even older stone arch spanning the river. Known locally as 'Roman Bridge', it is probably a medieval packhorse bridge which carried those using this route over Afon Machno. The rivers in this area provided a major obstacle to early travellers and numerous bridges like this one would have been built to aid their passage. From here, travellers would have continued down to Afon Lledr, to pass through Betws-y-Coed and on through the mountains.

The existence of the hospice at Ysbyty Ifan a few miles to the east, indicates that pilgrims came this way en-route to Bardsey throughout the Middle Ages. The hospice was established by the 'Knights of the Order of St John of Jerusalem' in the closing years of the twelfth century, to provide rest and refuge in what would have then been a wild and remote area. The hospice continued to be used until the Dissolution in the sixteenth century. By this time it had become notorious as the abode of outlaws and thieves wishing to avoid justice.

The nearby mill was built in the 1830s as a 'pandy' or 'fulling' mill similar to the mill at Trefriw. It was used to finish cloth woven on nearby farms by means of large fulling hammers driven by a water wheel. The mill remained a family run enterprise until the 1960s, when it was sold to the present owners who have turned it into a craft centre.

Continue along the lane to the first forestry road on the left (about 200 yards). Turn sharp left here and follow the road uphill.

(If the rivers are full it is worth making a short detour to the Machno Falls. These can be reached by continuing along the lane for another 400 yards or so to a house on the left called 'Pandy'. The falls lie directly opposite the house, but take care as there is no fencing. Return to this point to continue the walk.)

The forestry road is bordered by beech trees at first and after about 400 yards begins to curve rightwards. Immediately after the second bend and before a fork, bear right onto an unmade track which rises gently to a large metal gate. Go through the gate and keep right following a narrow path to join a track at a T junction. Turn right here and follow the track past the farmhouse of Coed-y-Ffynnon.

This ancient building, now rather run down and in need of repair, dates from the sixteenth century and was used for a time as a nunnery. At the turn of the century Lord Banks, a Lord Chief Justice, used it as a hunting lodge and constructed the nearby 'Panorama Drive' for his guests, which in the days before the conifer plantations, would have given magnificent views of the Conwy Valley and the mountains of Snowdonia.

The house stands close to the site of a medieval chapel, famous for the healing waters of its well (after which the house is named). A nearby stone, known as 'maen siglo' —the 'shaking stone', was said to shake when the bell in the tiny chapel rang.

2. Beyond the house the track enters the conifer plantations by a large gate. This is the start of the 'Panorama Drive' but the trees now screen any view. About 50 yards into the woods, turn left onto a faint footpath marked by a yellow arrow. This takes a direct line through the trees and is indicated by yellow paint marks. After about 150 yards, join a faint track which shortly narrows into a footpath again. Fallen trees block the path here and there and finding the correct route can be difficult, so keep looking for the paint marks.

At a break in the pine trees, bear right for a few yards, then curve left uphill following the paint marks. At the top of the rise, cross the remains of a low stone wall on the left and walk straight ahead to join a forestry track after about 150 yards or so (don't worry too much if you miss the wall;

Roman Bridge

if you walk straight ahead at the top of the rise, you will reach the forest track anyway). Turn left and follow the track to a T junction adjacent to a clearing, where gravel is being removed and stored. Turn right here and follow a much more pronounced forestry road. As the road bends left down the hill, fine views begin to open out of the Conwy Valley and the mountains of Snowdonia.

The best viewpoint is immediately above an area of felled trees, which gives fine views down into the Conwy Valley and west to the higher peaks of Snowdonia. Moel Siabod is the nearest and most prominent peak, with Snowdon just visible to the left. Northwards, the panorama takes in the Glyders, with the triple summit of Tryfan peeping over the shoulder of Galt-yr-Ogof and the softer contours of the Carneddau.

Continue down the forest road to a junction. Here a well used road bears left uphill to the farm of Fedw Deg. Directly opposite is a rather less obvious track, which drops diagonally down the hillside to the right. Turn right here and follow the path, overgrown but still clearly in use to the lane at the bottom of the hill.

This is known as the 'path of Gruffydd ap Dafydd Goch' and was the original access route to the ancient house of Fedw Deg. Gruffydd ap Dafydd Goch was the great-great-grandson of Llywelyn Fawr and a distinguished local knight who fought in the French Wars of Edward III under the Black Prince. He lived at Fedw Deg until his death and is buried at St Michael's church in Betws-y-Coed, where a fine stone effigy (1380) can be seen of him in full armour. It was his grandson Dafydd, who sold the nearby Gwydir estate to the Wynn family about 1500.

3. Turn left along the lane passing a row of stone cottages and at the next junction keep right down the hill. Cross the bridge over Afon Lledr and turn right along the main road. Take care on this section as the road has no footpath and can be busy. Turn right over the bridge (Pont yr Afanc) and immediately before the Fairy Glen Hotel turn right onto an unmade track, signposted 'Fairy Glen'. Walk up the track to a gate, where a short detour can be made to one of the most famous beauty spots in the locality—Fairy Glen. A small fee is payable. Return to this point to complete the walk.

Fairy Glen became popular and acquired its name during the Victorian period when Thomas Telford's new road allowed the nearby town of Betws-y-Coed to develop as a tourist destination. The original Welsh name—Ffos Noddyn—meaning 'deep chasm' or 'ditch', provides a more descriptive name than that of the romantic Victorians.

Continue up the track for almost one mile.

This was the original toll road between Betws-y-Coed and Pentrefoelas, built by the Capel Curig Turnpike Trust in the opening years of the nineteenth century. It provided a link between an earlier

98

toll road which came to Pentrefoelas but then headed north to Llanrwst via Nebo and the road constructed by Lord Penrhyn through the Ogwen Valley, linking Bangor to the mines above Ty Hyll (the 'Ugly House' on what is now the A5). It crossed Afon Conwy at Pont yr Afanc (which we have just crossed), now used by the A470 Lledr Valley road and continued through Betws-y-Coed, thus providing a route through the mountains for the London to Holyhead road, which avoided all the problems encountered on the coastal route via Conwy.

Stone embankments and buttresses can still be seen higher up above the Conwy Falls but it was still very narrow (rarely more than eight feet!) and the gradient was steep, making it both difficult and dangerous for coaches. It became redundant in 1815 when Thomas Telford built what is now the A5. Telford took a line higher up the hillside which was less steep (never more than 1 : 22) but he found the section above the Conwy Falls to be the most difficult of the entire route through the mountains.

Telford's road is now the A5 and has remained virtually unaltered. It is still the main route through the mountains of Snowdonia and has stood the test of time, despite almost 80 years of increasingly heavy motor traffic.

At the road turn right and return to the Conwy Falls Cafe and Restaurant.

Mara Publications

Mara Publications publish a range of walking guides and have the following list to date:

A Walker's Guide to the Wirral Shore Way
ISBN 0 9522409 0 4. This book describes a linear walk of over 20 miles following Wirral's old coastline between Chester and Hoylake.

Circular Walks along the Sandstone Trail
ISBN 0 9522409 2 0. The Sandstone Trail is Cheshire's best known and most popular walking route. This book gives a complete route description along with 12 circular walks.

Walking in Wirral   ISBN 0 9522409 1 2.
A collection of 12 circular walks in Wirral.

Walking in the Clwydian Hills and the Vale of Llangollen
ISBN 0 9522409 3 9. A collection of circular walks in the beautiful hills and valleys of the Welsh borders.

Circular Walks along the Gritstone Trail and Mow Cop Trail
ISBN 0 9522409 4 7. A route which follows Cheshire's eastern border along the edge of the Peak District. Following the same format as the Sandstone Trail book—a full route description for both trails is combined with 12 circular walks.

Coastal Walks around Anglesey
ISBN 0 9522409 6 3. A collection of 15 walks which explore the varied scenery of Anglesey's beautiful coastline.

Forthcoming book:
Walking in Lleyn—Exploring the Coast and Hills
ISBN 0 9522409 5 5. A collection of 15 walks on the coast and hills of the Lleyn Peninsula.